WHISPERS
FROM A LOVING GOD

For Luke & Crystal
Wishing you Hope in the morning,
Joy in the moment
and
Victory through Surrender
in Christ,

Love Karen

961-5209

Karen Petty Felton

CROSSBOOKS
PUBLISHING

CrossBooks™
A Division of LifeWay
1663 Liberty Drive
Bloomington, IN 47403
www.crossbooks.com
Phone: 1-866-879-0502

First published by CrossBooks 3/14/2011

ISBN: 978-1-6150-7754-0 (sc)
ISBN: 978-1-6150-7755-7 (dj)

Library of Congress Control Number: 2011923044

Printed in the United States of America

This book is printed on acid-free paper.

Any people depicted in stock imagery provided by Thinkstock are models,
and such images are being used for illustrative purposes only.

Certain stock imagery © Thinkstock.

For my children, Libby and Michael, you are my symphony.

For my little sister Patti, you are the lifter of my head.
For my friends, you are the cha-cha in my chocolate.
For my husband, Mike, you are my Big Fish
and ever shall be
my Hero.

When writing songs of good, great men,
Of heroes and their day,
we write of battles with dragons bold,
and mythical, magical things,
and sailors who claim their bounty
on oceans with sails as their wings.

Some write of battles fought,
of heroes bold, of wisdom wrought.
I write this song of a godly man,
who sails through life as the ocean.
My hero, my husband, my friend,
whose compass is God,
whose flame is love.
The wind in his sails is devotion.

Love and blessings, Karen

Preface

It is through the clarity and distance of time that I now peer into my past, feeling safe to experience again through memory those things which have made me the person I am today. As I consider my life and the individual tragedies of my soul, I have come to understand more clearly the tenderness, love, and compassion of my God.

In considering the crimes against my body and spirit, I see a small child, a life of tragedies and miracles. I will not discuss any intimate details of my abuses; it is enough that I found victory over those circumstances. I will endeavor to focus on the positive aspects of my life. I will focus on the love and hope that I found in my Jesus.

Recovery and victory have sometimes felt more alien to me than a cancer eating away at my heart. When depression overwhelms a heart, it is *hope* that takes the hardest blow. It is the very concept of hope that causes the heart to ache, sometimes more than the violations themselves.

When embracing hope, we submit to vulnerability long ago rejected. It is this vulnerability that I have come to understand as true strength—a strength and peace that surpasses all understanding. Without the living waters of hope, I would have long ago withered and died. My eternal hope is in Christ.

I write this book to celebrate the person whom God has created. I choose not to condemn or judge those who harmed me. It is the love of my Christ on which I choose to stand.

As I consider my life, I have come to realize that I have done nothing of consequence. I am fifty-five years old; there is nothing special about me. I am okay with that. As the saying goes, "She is special, but her name ain't

Ed." I have done a little bit of everything and a whole lot of nothing, but oh how God loves me.

I am victorious over a childhood of abuse, abandonment, neglect, and violence against every fiber of my being. I emerged on the living side of a ten-year battle with depression that included twenty-five shock treatments and nearly resulted in a lobotomy. At the age of thirty-five, I developed advanced early-onset Parkinson's disease and was bound to wheelchair and bed within five years.

I added it up the other day: eighteen years of abuse, trusting no one; ten years of horrible depression, self-abuse, and suicidal behaviors; and twenty years of Parkinson's disease. That is forty-eight out of fifty-five years of my life.

Through it all has been my husband and friend—sometimes shell-shocked, yet always my friend and fortress. He recently remarked that his faith has been shaken by witnessing everything I have been through. He said he did not know how I could praise God in all my writings and teachings. He said the only grace he sees is in how I handle my life.

I told him that he makes God's grace manifest in my life every day. "Where do you think that grace comes from?" I asked him.

Life is about challenges and choices. We may not have a choice about the challenges we face, but we do have a choice about how we face them. I choose to trust God, seek joy, live boldly, and love abundantly.

To God be the glory!

Contents

Key to Illustrations

Chapter One
Trust God Introduction

"Trust in the Lord with all your heart and lean not on your own understanding" (Prov. 3:5).

My entire life has been a lesson in trusting God. I am convinced that, even before I was aware of God, his heart was with me, that he loved me when no one else cared. This is evidenced by my survival in a horrendous environment, surviving what I believe was encephalitis as an infant left unattended in an attic and exposed to nearly fatal amounts of mosquito venom.

Growing up abused in every fashion, the world taught me that I could not trust the people I could see. How was I to trust a god I could *not* see? Again and again, God whispered, "Trust me," until at eighteen I left home.

I was still in high school; I had no job, no place to live. I did not know what the future held. I simply knew that I could no longer tolerate the sin in my birth family. I learned to trust God through teachers, principals, and eventually, my husband.

When I was thirty-five, God again whispered, "Trust me." I began my twenty-year journey with Parkinson's disease. I have heard that a journey of a thousand miles begins with a single footstep. I think it begins with an argument over how to pack the suitcase.

For twenty years, God and I have been wrestling—sometimes toe-to-toe, up close and personal—over how, and with what, to pack my suitcase. My plans were not always God's plans.

He has stilled the rages in my heart and calmed the anger, fear, and pain in my mind and body. God has proved, time and again, that he can take my anger, uncertainties, and sorrows. He loves me. He is unfaltering—*unfaltering*—and infinitely, eternally holy. In all things, my loving Father, my Abba, my God, I trust you.

Trust God

"I love you, O Lord, my strength. The Lord is my rock, my fortress and my deliverer; my God is my rock, in whom I take refuge. He is my shield and the horn of my salvation, my stronghold. I call to the Lord, who is worthy of praise" (Ps. 18:1–3).

Old Farm House – watercolor, circa 1974

Courage to Live, 1988

Standing on the front porch of the house and looking through the doorway, I began to face the pain. The house had seemed so big before, so evil. My memory carried me back. I was a little girl again, whose pain and shame were quieted by the doors of the house and the fear of being discovered.

The paint was weathered, the windows were broken, and most of the doors were off their hinges. When it was my house, it was filled with children. I was the oldest girl of alcoholic and abusive parents. I grew up learning that I was not worthy of even the simplest of pleasures—smiling. To smile was to invite ridicule and punishment. I learned instead that happiness was only for those who deserved it, and that my only function was to keep the secrets.

"Just go ahead and do it" and "don't tell" were the words I remembered most. They echoed through my mind as I stood in the doorway of my old room. The room seemed much smaller now. My feelings of late were not those of a thirty-year-old woman but of a child, a victim of the worst kind. The feelings were those of a child who just wanted to be held and to hear those words coming from another soul: "It'll be all right." I had said them to myself over and over throughout my childhood—after being kicked and beaten, after the crimes against my body and my spirit. I would huddle, cradled in my own arms, and repeated over and over, "It'll be all right."

Now, standing in that doorway, I heard myself saying those words—not as a child, but as a woman: "It'll be all right." Through my trip to this house—the place of my torture—God turned me away from being an instrument of suicide and vengeance. I would choose life. Standing on those rotted floors and hearing the echoes of the defiant screams of a child, "You can't hurt me!," I remembered the child who would not be defeated, who knew that she could not stop them from touching her body but vowed that they would never touch her soul. Standing in that house, I remembered her courage.

I stood in my old bedroom with the evening air blowing through the broken windows. I looked down at the rotted floor and the earth beneath it. I looked up and saw the closet, my hiding place. I would run to it to hide from my abusers. To my astonishment, it was not the enormous haven I remembered, the place in which I could protect myself. It measured only about two feet square. I realized that no child could have hidden there.

Standing in that doorway, I looked in on myself and remembered again the tears of a spirit so tender and vulnerable. I began to face the shame and fear. I began to see myself through God's eyes.

As I turned to leave, I looked back, and for a moment I remembered and heard again the voices of the children who had lived in this house. I heard their cries and their laughter. I was touched again by the young souls who tried so desperately to hold on. I was filled with the hope and courage of the child that is within me. It was enough that I stood in that doorway, held myself, and wept. It will be all right.

Trust God

"But I trust in your unfailing love; my heart rejoices in your salvation. I will sing to the Lord, for he has been good to me" (Ps. 13:5–6).

I am content with where God has brought me. I wish I were healthy. I wish the little girl I was could have been loved and nurtured the way God intended. But I am happy with where God has me today, with our relationship.

What are the desires of your heart?

God loves you so very much. He has suffered with us and for us throughout every difficult time in our lives. Is there a painful memory that God shares with you? Release that pain into the hands and heart of the great healer and, through Christ, be free.

Forest Moment – watercolor, circa 1978

As a teenager I faced daily beatings and abuses, and I would often run to the forest to find God's comfort. I received the following gift from God when I was thirteen.

Forest Moment
October 14, 1987

The earth gave up another season. The girl stood hiding among the trees, knowing that in a moment the fawn would leave her. It stood tall, ears straining for the sound, the danger. In all of time, the girl knew there would never be another moment like this.

She waited; she watched; and as the leaves fell around it, all she could see was its leaving.

The silence gave way to the rustling wind, and the fawn moved deeper into the forest. The girl, with each breath, moved with the fawn. Every muscle straining, reaching, grasping the earth that held her to it. She knew that were it not for the earth that held her to it, she and the fawn would take flight.

They strode easily over every obstacle, pacing themselves, sharing the wind, hearts pounding, muscles unyielding, spirits growing stronger, becoming more like the other than themselves. And they ran on.

With each moment, each stride, reality grew stronger, pulling the girl from the fawn and the fawn from the girl. With unspoken words, their journey ended.

Their hearts, stilled by their parting, each moved silently into their own worlds—the girl toward home, the fawn toward the protection of the forest. The moments they shared would never be forgotten.

Trust God

"As the deer pants for streams of water, so my soul pants for you, O God. My soul thirsts for God, the living God. When can I go and meet with God?" (Ps. 42:1).

When we are in need, God is there, waiting. We must only look around to see him. When was the last time you ran to your room in eager anticipation of your time in prayer with God? What could you change to spend more time in God's lap?

Cherished Losses

It was through the grace of God that I was saved as a seven-year-old child. I knew very little about God—simply that I loved him because he loved me. Someone recently asked me why I loved my earthly father. I answered them saying, "Well, he is my father." I do not say this to diminish my parents in any fashion. They were simply products of their heritage—a heritage that I would have shared had it not been for the very real love that I felt from my heavenly Father, my Abba.

This next story I share is not a confession. I confessed this sin over thirty-six years ago in the darkness of my bedroom. I am telling this story to praise God for teaching a little girl right from wrong when others around me were leading me away from God and into sin. Thirty-six years ago, this sin was confessed and forgiven, but I have carried the evidence of that sin for a long time.

My father was a thief, a convict, and I loved him. One night, he came home and told our family that some people were moving and that they were going to let us have anything we wanted from their home. I remember that the house was very nice; it was filled with beautiful things. It was very dark in the house. My brothers and sister were running and grabbing things, and I was scared. I was seven years old—I could barely read—and that night I stole four Bobbsey Twins books.

My family quickly left the home of these strangers with our treasures. I do not remember anything else that was stolen by my family that night—only the books that I carried with me.

Later, as I lay in my bed in the darkness of my room, I cried because I felt guilty and alone.

I asked my mother, "Momma, did we do something wrong tonight?"

"No," was her answer.
"Momma, did we steal those things tonight?" I asked.
"No," was again the answer.

Momma left, and I could see her standing in the light of the doorway. I could hear the breathing of my brothers and sister who shared a bed with me, and I was frightened and alone. I know now that the loneliness I felt was separation from God. To a seven-year-old child, it was simply the shame of knowing that I was a thief. I had stolen something from another child.

That night I asked God to forgive me: "I'm sorry, God. I'm so sorry for what I did. Please tell me what to do." God was very real to me. I knew he still loved me, and I knew in my heart that I was forgiven. However, I did not know what to do with the books, so I kept them.

For the next eleven years, God was my only comfort. Satan had built a fortress around my birth family, and I was subjected to abuses that would have destroyed me had I not known God.

Many times as I hid, my young body bruised and violated, I would cry to God to help me, and I could feel his arms around me. I could hear him say, "I am here. It will be all right." I longed for the innocence stolen from me so long ago. In a desert of tears, Christ was my oasis of hope.

Ten days after my eighteenth birthday, I ran away from home. I had very little money and nowhere safe to hide—only a few clothes and those four books. In the years since then, I have lived in runaway shelters in the homes of loving people who opened their hearts and homes to me. I have rented my own apartments. I graduated from high school and from college. I met and married my husband and was blessed with two wonderful children. There were times when my husband and I were in college that we sold many of our valued possessions simply to eat. I did not sell the books. I considered throwing them away or donating them to a fundraiser for charity. They were very old books and I suspected they might have been of some value.

In the thirty-six years that I have had the books, I have never read them. I have cared for them even though they represented a part of myself that I would and did hide from others for a very long time. I protected the books and cherished them as a symbol of God's love and forgiveness. The books were a secret between God and myself, hidden behind other books on our shelves, never belonging to me or to the young girl from whom they were stolen so many years ago.

Why was I holding onto the evidence of a sin so long ago forgiven? Many things were stolen from me in my childhood; the most longed-for was my innocence. I have often wondered about what I stole as a child from a child.

There are times when we can only wait for God to reveal himself. In the matter of four stolen books, he would wait over thirty-six years. As I sat at a table having breakfast with ladies from my church, we discussed our excitement about the retreat we were attending, the remarkable testimonies we'd heard, and how God had brought us all together.

The conversation then turned to our fears. I listened as a good friend shared how fearful she was, and often is, as a result of being burglarized as a child. She shared things stolen in a time of innocence. At that moment, only God and I knew of the bond we shared. I hadn't stolen the books from *her*, yet I shared in the sin of those who had stolen from her. The decision required no prayer time, only a step of faith and a gift from God.

My friend and I spoke of God's love, his forgiveness, and his grace. We spoke of shared losses and the burdens of stolen innocence, and I knew the books should belong to her. In presenting the books to my friend, I hoped to give her the message that her possessions and her innocence had not been lost. Instead they had been guarded, protected, and cherished by God, to be presented to her in love. In releasing the books, God allowed me to rejoice in the knowledge that God's will, God's grace, and God's love will shine through.

I do not know what God has planned for the books or the end to this story. I am certain that he brought two women together to heal our hearts and help us to regain and set free our cherished losses.

Trust God

"Do not let sin reign in your mortal body so that you obey its evil desires" (Rom. 6:12).

What sin do you hide away from the world? Have you confessed that sin before God? If the answer is no, do this now. If the answer is yes, you have been forgiven and made clean from sin's penalty through Jesus Christ.

Has something been stolen from you? Does your heart ache from the loss of hope? No matter what the enemy has done to you or through you, God can make it right. He guards those losses so tenderly because he loves you. He was with you every step of every heartache. It's time now to set free your cherished losses; your sins and heartache can be set free. We only need to ask him and allow him.

Accept the bad things, but do not embrace them. Do not allow them to become part of you.

If we as victims of sin allow that darkness into our hearts, Satan wins. We will then carry in our hearts those dark memories, as well as the feelings of anger, hatred, self-loathing, and depression.

What losses have you been carrying that you now present to God?

Fearfully and Wonderfully Made

Read Psalms 138 and 139.

Does God fear? Those words imply that God does fear. If so, what is the basis of that fear?

I begin with the full and certain knowledge that God loves me. Because of the limitations of my humanity, I am sure that I may never comprehend the scope of his love or the depth of his compassion for me. I try to rest upon the certain knowledge of his love and compassion every moment of every day.

Tonight I was awakened with these questions: Where do I fit in God's plan? How does my suffering glorify God? What did God fear when he fashioned this life for me? I do not imagine that God lies awake with the same fears as ours. So many of us try to fit God into our meager vocabulary. We try to use words to describe the indescribable.

To understand the concept of being "fearfully made," I must ask myself, what does God fear? What did he fear when he made me?

I believe that God's fear is based on his compassion for us. Knowing the life he himself ordained for me long before my birth, I know that God feared for me. I read Psalms 138 and 139, and I stand in awe of God's love for me. What incredible love, powerful grace, and abiding sense of purpose he has for each of our lives. How deep is his love for us, to have set each life into his perfect plan?

As a parent, I know of the dreams we fashion for our children. My hopes and plans were of health and joy for both my children. My plans for my children began long before their births and were amplified when I held them and looked into their eyes. What joy and hope and overwhelming love!

I try to imagine God forming my hands and feet. I wonder what he must have been thinking as I opened my eyes for the first time, and he peered into my very soul (Ps. 139:16). What pride, what love he must feel for us, perhaps to be held in his holy hand for only an instant. In his abundant love and perfect plan, he places each of us into this foul, sinful world.

He loved this little, brown-eyed girl so perfectly and tenderly, knowing intensely and intimately the suffering she would endure. Yet he had the vision and will to place all things—good and bad—in my life for a purpose. This is the true scope of God's love for each of us.

In suffering, I have witnessed the scope of his mercy. In being served by others, I have seen the reflection of his compassion. In facing my own mortality and physical frailties, I have come to know the wealth of his grace.

Pain creates a form of loneliness that no human bond can breach. Daily I drink from the cup of agony. I know too well the familiar taste of pain and brokenness that carry both blessing and sorrow. In these most desperate and familiar times, my walk with God has been the sweetest and most intimate.

Having his love and comfort during these times has brought clarity of vision and perspective of God's purpose for the cross. It has fostered in me a compassion for my Christ beyond the written word. If it were only my own sin that nailed my Christ to the cross, he would still have lovingly offered himself up for me.

If it were only my sin that caused God to turn away from Christ and be separated for the first time in eternity, then God and his son Jesus would still have fulfilled their purpose.

What incredible love, what powerful grace, what abiding purpose God revealed in Christ's suffering. It is because of the cross and the love that was nailed there that none of us ever have to suffer the loneliness that Christ suffered. None of us need ever be separated from God.

God's fear does not lie in weakness. It lives in the depth of his love and the height of his compassion.

Trust God

The knowledge that God is in control and that through him we will be victorious over all hardships frees our lives from worry so that we might have joy overflowing.

"Consider it pure joy, my brothers, whenever you face trials of many kinds, because you know that the testing of your faith develops perseverance. Perseverance must finish its work so that you may be mature and complete, not lacking anything" (James 1:2–4).

When Christ faced his own pain on the cross, he did so with prayer to his Father. He asked to have the cup taken from him but bowed to the will of his Father.

What pure joy are you ready to accept? Are you ready today to accept the ultimate joy—life eternal with God? I can hardly wait.

Dear God,

I went to see my brother Jeff today. It is difficult to separate my concerns for today from memories that linger in the shadows of my heart. Jeff recently emerged from a coma. He wanted me to have power of attorney and to arrange his health care directive. I have lived my life based on accomplishments and goals. I make lists of tasks and mark them off like items that go into a shopping cart. I had my list of things that Jeff needed done. I was ready to get things in order.

For most of our lives, Jeff and I were at odds with each other. We competed greedily for whatever crumbs of affection might fall our way. Jeff's mistake was in looking for crumbs from our family, and he found no nourishment. Eventually, he found nourishment in self-medicating and drugs. I sought nourishment from my Bible, teachers, my art, and friends.

For so many years, I have known and remembered my brother in his mental illness. I carry with me memories of a childhood where dysfunction was the norm. A normal day for me included neglect, abuse, oatmeal for breakfast, an older brother who was my hero, a younger sister who never got hit, and Jeff. Jeff was an outcast even in our own sick family.

Today in the hospital, I saw more of my brother than I have in years. It was so easy to think that Jeff's mind had been stolen years ago, and that all he had left was the tragedy that I knew and remembered. I was wrong. Nothing in life is as simple as it seems. Jeff is dying; he is paranoid-schizophrenic and alcoholic, has AIDS and liver failure, and he is my little brother.

Gone were the wild, glazed eyes that I had looked into for so many years. Instead, I found myself looking into the dark, gentle eyes of my brother. "Please don't drink anymore," I pleaded.

His tragic wisdom broke my heart. "I just wanted to share something with someone."

My heart began to feel the loneliness and weight of his world. I sat there for a few uncomfortable moments, not doing or saying anything. Jeff comforted me. "It'll be all right, Sis." I made some joke, trying not to feel or see the pity of it all. He said he loved Jesus and that everything would be all right.

For so long my prayer had been that Jeff had accepted the Lord and that someday, in heaven, I would finally know that man that God had intended to be my brother. Today, God allowed me to peer into the eyes of that man. I asked him when he had been saved. He told me it was a long time ago and that he had done some backsliding since then. I told him I backslide every time I get out of bed. I left his room, not understanding our new roles. God helped me to leave behind the role of the strong sister and to simply be the loving sister. After today, I hope to go back to the hospital to hug my brother, hold his hand, and like Christ, simply and truly love him.

Footnote: Jeff recovered from his coma, and as of October 2010, he has lived with full-blown AIDS for over fifteen years. He is fighting a good fight in his battle against mental illness.

Are you keeping so busy that you can't feel or experience the power of God's love and redemption? My brother sought emotional nourishment and fulfillment from the wrong sources—his family. To whom do you look for validation?

Trust God

In John 6:35, Jesus said, "I am the bread of life. He who comes to me will never go hungry, and he who believes in me will never be thirsty." Where can we turn for true spiritual nourishment?

The woman in Matthew 15:27 said, "Yes, Lord, but even the dogs eat the crumbs that fall from their masters' table." God is infinite; he cares for us deeply and desires nothing from us other than our fellowship and praise.

Solitude

The corner's there.
The woman's there.
The child's not far behind.
She beckons—hands,
Come on, sweetheart.
And leading on round
Corners dark,
She comes back
Near
The child in
Fear
Laid down with angry hands,
Child reaches out with pleading eyes
To hearts whose souls
Are dead with lies.

There is an evil force in this world that we humans are ill-equipped to handle. If we as believers expect to have an easy victory, we are mistaken. Only Christ can battle the powers of Satan, and prayer is the only sword we can wield.

I faced evil on a daily basis as a child. I had no one to pray with me; however, I am certain that my Mimmaw and Grammaw Guthrie prayed for me. I wrote the poem above twenty years ago while dealing with depression and issues of sexual abuse as a child.

The rest of the poem is fairly graphic and is not included, but those last two lines are the important part. Anyone who abuses a child sexually has a dead soul. Their soul has been destroyed by Satan's lies. Be ever watchful over your children; be ever vigilant in your prayers for your children, and love them ever so tenderly.

Trust God

"And the King shall answer and say unto them, 'Verily I say unto you, in as much as ye have done it unto one of the least of these brethren, ye have done it unto me" (Matt. 25:40).

Do you know anyone who needs you to pray boldly for them?

Tough Times

The Bible does not promise a life of ease if you are a believer. Quite the contrary, God's word reveals time and again that we rarely grow through uneventful lives. It is through discord, hardships, adversity, and tragedy that we grow and are perfected. Our salvation and God's purpose for the cross illustrate that principle. We are not bought with kindness. Indeed, Christ's love was a key factor, but the defining cost of our eternal salvation was Christ's blood.

I do not, by any stretch of conscience or intellect, believe that God caused or sanctioned my abuse. I do know that he was with me, shielding me and enabling me during each and every moment. I know he protected me by hiding some terrible memories from me for decades.

Even in the darkest of times, when keeping secrets was my directive, God was helping my heart and mind to understand, to overcome. He gave me a love of poetry and the ability and desire to express myself— even my darkest self—through my writings and artwork.

God is good.

The Kite Catcher

March 18, 1988

Bitter dreams
of yesterday
Catch the soul,
whose flight did stay.
Soaring high, the passerby
Did grasp and hold
till breathless dawn
The heart that dreamed
But never did fly.
The tree, this rooted passerby,
Did grasp my kite and held it down,
Till breathless struggles,
Wind and rain,
will not my kite be flown again?

Splendor – 1984

Shadow of leaves hiding danger
Shades the face
Of a deadly stranger.
Arms of timber reaching out
Grasping death
And my soul without
Branches long and branches lean
Came so slowly
Death I've seen
All within a moment's splendor
I have come and
Been condemned there.

Trust God

"I will lead her into the desert and speak tenderly to her" (Hos. 2:14).

How has God comforted and taught you during a difficult time?

Beyond Victory

When speaking of recovery, a lot of emphasis these days is on the word survivor—as though the word were itself a beacon of hope and healing meant to guide us through even the darkest of times. I challenge you to move beyond words like *overcomer, victor,* and *survivor.*

A wounded animal survives a battle by crawling off and licking it's wounds. A victor has wounds but chooses to carry on without nurturing them.

A victor dances without legs, flies without wings, sings without a voice, touches the stars without hands, loves beyond measure, and embraces God with every beat of his heart. We can have victory today by choosing to focus on the positive. This requires an active pursuit of joy, of God.

People are always blaming God when things go wrong in their lives. Where is the blame that Satan carries? God did not create disease and heartache. Only the enemy flourishes in doubt and blaming God.

We can have victory through righteous anger. So get angry. Even Christ got angry and tossed a few tables over. But do not sin in your anger. To violate another person—victim or perpetrator—is wrong. Wrong is wrong. We as believers in and followers of Christ carry a deeper challenge. That challenge is the mission of our Christ—to save that which is lost.

Of course, it is not your mission or purpose to save your perpetrator. That is God's purpose, Christ's job. Your job is to move beyond your perpetrator, past the pain and denial. Your task is to accept the bad things that happened to you but not embrace them. Do not hold so tightly to the negative that you can't reach out and lift your voice to worship God or to sing "then sings my soul, my Savior God to thee, how great thou art."

We all have times when our faith flops around like a fish out of water. The true picture of who we are as believers comes in those moments of turning back to God's will. We can follow our Christ's example as he prayed in the garden, "Father, take this cup from me," but who then added, "Father, thy will, not mine be done." (Matt. 14:36).

Trust God

We all have issues that need to be given to God. We live in a fallen world, and no one will get through this life without pain. Sometimes our pain is more familiar to us than life without it.

Is there a wound you have been nurturing?
Now is the time to release your heartache to God.

Love Lived in Imboden, Arkansas

I think back and wonder how I could have survived the abuse, neglect, and violence outside of Imboden, Arkansas. There was no safe place for me.

I thank God for my memories of Imboden. I choose to accept the bad things that have happened, but not to embrace them. Instead, I choose to be a reflection of the love and faith in God that I found in Imboden.
I knew a place of love and laughter.
I knew where God lived.
I knew where love lived.
Love lived in Imboden.

My Grammaw, Mimmaw as I knew her, was somewhat of a rowdy gal in her youth, from what I was told. She was a Blue Bonnet Girl, sang on country radio, and drove a big rig truck. Aunt Ruby told me that Mimmaw could back those huge old cars up onto the tandem truck better and faster than any man around.

I cherished every moment with Mimmaw. For a while, she cared for the four of us as her own children. Mimmaw Pat walked us to church every Sunday. We were always dressed and polished. She waited for us outside and walked us proudly home. It was in that church one Sunday morning that I gave my heart and life to Jesus Christ. Thank you, Mimmaw.

I remember she would take me with her on long car rides on the back roads of Arkansas. I can still hear the crunch of gravel under the tires. I love that sound. She delivered jars of tea to gentlemen who lived on these roads. My Mimmaw made the best tea in Arkansas and was a popular gal.

I would stay in the car under the shade of some old tree while she went to the porch and had a sip of her finest teas with these gentlemen and occasionally a lady or two. We would quickly be on our way.

My Grammaw was instrumental in my salvation. She walked us to church, but to my knowledge she never went in. I do not know if Mimmaw was saved, but I hope and pray that she is in heaven waiting for me. My hope is that at some point she made peace with God.

Who does your heart worry about? Our ultimate hope is in Christ.

Trust God

Matthew 20:1–18 refers to salvation gained in the eleventh hour of life. What a wonderful promise of hope for believers and sinners alike. Who do you hope gained salvation in the eleventh hour?

The sidewalk lay outside the gate to Grammaw and Grampaw's house. The sidewalk led to all of Imboden, a magical place that grew mysteriously smaller the older we grew.

A Magical Place

Imboden, Arkansas, was a magical place—a place where a child could be anything. No authority or nation, except the imagination, could determine what each day held for us. The kingdom of Imboden began at the gate to Grammaw and Grampaw's yard. Outside the gate was the sidewalk, which led to all of Imboden, a kingdom that mysteriously grew smaller as we grew older.

The wonderful thing about magical kingdoms is that the people who inhabit them never really die. They live on in the hearts of those who loved them. The best thing about Grammaw and Grampaw is how they fostered the child within all of us. They encouraged us to dream, to imagine, to play. Their love was limitless.

When I remember Grampaw, I remember his gift of telling stories. Grampaw, P.Y. Guthrie, gave me the gift of embellishment. He could spin a yarn better than anyone I have ever known. He taught me how to gut a fish and gave me my first—and last—taste of chewing tobacco.

His theory was this: If you are with a group of kids, you can trick one of them; but if you divide, you conquer. For me, it was a special invitation to go with him to the livestock auction barn. We sat on the bed of his old truck, quietly talking, my short legs swinging loosely over the side.

He took a big chew off his tobacco cake and handed it to me. "Want a chaw?" he asked.

"Yeah, Grampaw!" I said.

"Don't tell Grammaw," he instructed softly as he passed me the tobacco. I eagerly and greedily took the biggest bite I could.

The tobacco came spewing out of my mouth a lot faster than it went in. I'll never forget the hot bitter taste.

"Don't care for tobaccie, eh?" he said. "Remember that." We sat for a while longer and talked about everything and nothing. Then we headed for home.

Grammaw Guthrie, "Gyp" as Grampaw affectionately called her, was a gentle, loving woman. She gave me the gift of living faith, of knowing that if you love someone, praying for them is a natural product of that love.

Trust God

"Be joyful always; pray continually; give thanks in all circumstances, for this is God's will for you in Christ Jesus" (1 Thess. 5:16–18).

Make a list of those you pray for without ceasing. I challenge you to add to that list monthly, if not weekly.

Summer of Sadness

The summer before my daughter's senior year of high school, I was given a heart-wrenching lesson in letting go and letting God. It began with the death of a sweet, larger-than-life girl at our church. I tried to make sense of her death for my daughter and her friends. I failed. I am convinced that there are some things our frail hearts were not meant to understand.

Two weeks later, another classmate was killed. I bought funeral clothes for some of her friends, and they promised me there would be no more funerals. A few days later, my daughter and her boyfriend of two years came into our bedroom. His head was bowed, and he quietly whispered, "Joey didn't keep his promise." Another of her friends had been killed. That evening, the local paper interviewed our youth group led by my daughter's boyfriend.

The title of the article was "Summer of Sadness." The paper ran a half-page photo of him raising his hands in prayer and praise. The next day the paper ran the same picture announcing his death in an auto accident. I remember he was a playful, funny boy.

When someone's child passes, it leaves a hole in us all and steals our breath. Letting go of our children to grow as God wills is where the rubber meets the road in parenting. It is what brings us to our knees and keeps us there.

A friend once wept that she didn't know where her stillborn infant's soul was. I assured her through scripture where that precious soul was. "Today you shall be with me in Paradise" (Luke 23:43) and "Absent from the body, present with the Lord" (2 Cor. 5:8).

Trust God

God always keeps his promises. You will be
reunited with your loved ones.

What is the first thing you would like to do in
heaven? Who would you like to do it with?
List three things and three people.

Your challenge: Take your list and find three
someones to do these things with.

"Precious in the sight of the Lord is the death of his faithful servants" (Ps. 116:15).

in perfect peace she lived
and walked among us
that we might grow and learn of love
with every breath we long to see her
every heartbeat cries to God above
so wonderful her smile, her gaze
that He should call her home

please linger near sweet memories
of precious yesterday
but for a moment , she stood near
and held our hearts
now this we pray

Oh Father God
hold her tenderly
till angels call me home
to embrace again this jewel
Your child
whose tender heart you gave me
she gave it back to you, her Christ
and now this life
sweet memory
is all that daily saves me.

(Those who go before us
leave us with bittersweet memories.
We who are left behind
carry those memories like precious jewels
until the day we are reunited.
We will throw off those memories
like schoolbooks on a playground,
replacing them with new
and wonderful adventures.)

Please Pray with Me ...

Of all the things I've been through, my brain surgery is one of the top five. For ten hours or so, I was totally in the surgeons hands. When the surgery began, I couldn't remember a single Bible verse or even the words to Jesus loves me. However, having taught the books of the Bible for over twenty years would shortly come in handy.

When I was told I would feel a tugging sensation, I knew they were peeling back my scalp. I began softly reciting: "Genesis, Exodus, Leviticus, Numbers ..." When they cut through my skull and drilled through my brain, I recited: "Genesis, Exodus, Leviticus, Numbers ..." With each step of surgery, I recited louder and faster. Knowing they were drilling into my brain was a bit overwhelming. Yet, oh how remarkable is our God to have created the human body, so fragile and strong, delicate and resilient. The brain, in all is complexity, feels no pain when cut.

Several years ago, a family member said to me, "Parkinson's disease isn't that bad. The fact is, only my husband knows my level of pain and disability. Always, God has been there. God is my fortress, my stronghold, my rock. Always, he is the lifter of my head.

In an e-mail to friends and family, I wrote: "I can't wait to see what tomorrow brings. I am starting a list of dreams, things I hope to do with my "resurrected" body. As you read this e-mail, I hope you will also complete the first item on my list, with me. I am going now to kneel in prayer for the first time in over six years. I am going to humble myself before him and be with my great and lovely God.

If you have ever prayed for me, I ask you now to pray *with* me.

Trust God

"I will proclaim the name of the Lord, ascribe greatness to our God, the Rock! His work is perfect" (Deut. 32:3).

Broken Vessels

About six months after my brain surgery, I fell in the kitchen and shattered my right shoulder. The recovery has taken over four years. I will probably never be pain-free because of it, but the pain is now manageable.

After two surgeries, the bone kept dying. It is amazing how quickly destiny can change a life. The pain I endured has been more than I could bear. The injury and pain from injury almost brought me to the end of me. I was in pain beyond description. I gained between thirty-five and fifty pounds of water weight. I was in diapers and could not walk a single step unassisted. I was on compression leg pumps twenty-four hours a day to fight edema.

My ankles would start out at nine inches in the morning, and by late afternoon they would swell to nineteen inches. I nicknamed the pump "my juicers." I believe my body was shutting down.

Trust God

The worldly view of something broken focuses on the uselessness of the object. The godly view is of repair and restoration. God can and will use everything, both broken and whole, to his glory. I wrote this song two months after my fall. Is there something in your life that God can repair, heal, or restore?

Have you ever felt truly broken? How did God use this brokenness?

Broken Vessels

April 4, 2007

Oh, Lord, my God,
My heart can understand
A vessel in its brokenness
Is useless to a man.
But Lord my God
How can this be
That this same vessel
Is most precious Lord to thee.

Oh broken vessel,
How can we sing,
How can our voices soar when
Silence steals our wings?
Oh broken vessel
Oh warrior my song

Karen Petty Felton

Alone and in your sorrows cry
With angels standing by
In that breathless moment
You changed the course of destiny
Replaced my sin and sorrows
Your love set me free.

Oh, Lord, my God,
My heart can understand
A vessel in its brokenness
Is useless to a man.
But Lord my God
How can this be
That this same vessel
Is most precious Lord to thee.

Trust God

"He heals the brokenhearted and binds up their wounds. He determines the number of the stars and calls them each by name" (Ps. 147:3–4).

I Stopped Counting at Five Hundred

October 26, 2008

After my brain surgery in 2006, I was filled with hope of a new day. In February of 2007, I fell in my kitchen and suffered a horrendous break in my shoulder. The pain was beyond what is humanly bearable, and yet my will to find purpose in my life would only challenge me further.

After making over 750 sparrow and bluebird pins, I began sewing quilted blankets. They were not what I call heirloom quilts like Grammaw put hours and hours of time into. My blankets are quite colorful and functional, and I pray as I make each blanket. In December 2007, I started putting blankets into matching pillowcases. This made the blankets more portable for everyone. I have made over 590 blankets.

My heart's desire is to go on mission trips, but that is not possible. My body, voice, and everything else are all too weak for a mission trip. God has used people who have given blankets to the homeless here in Missouri and lepers in India and Africa.

Now they daily look at my blankets that add color and beauty to drab and barren walls. It is my prayer that the people who receive the blankets also receive God's comfort and blessings. My blankets were used to teach the creation story and were presented with love to people in Russia, Moldova, Africa, India, and the homeless.

The whole time I was making my blankets, Satan was telling me what a stupid, pitiful life I had and what a joke I was. I battled thoughts of suicide daily.

I think back over the past year and a half. The pain I have endured has tested me more than I can possibly describe. As I think back, I can now see God's grace and hand in it all. Had I not broken my shoulder, I would not have met hundreds of people, doctors, therapists, and patients. My blankets have blessed so many. I cannot remember why I started sewing, only that I felt compelled to sew. Had I not developed speech problems, I would not have written this book or most of the praise songs and poems.

Trust God

"And we know that in all things God works for the good of those who love him, who have been called according to his purpose" (Rom. 8:28).

The Struggle Continues

October 28, 2008
E-mail sent to friends and family

Where do I begin? Tonight I spend my last night in St. Mary's Rehab for another surgery, my seventh in two years, this time for shoulder replacement. I have been so tremendously blessed by everyone here and by my church family and friends. I am overwhelmed. I think back over the past two years and feel as though I have been on a roller coaster ride. For those who did not know, the bone in my shoulder was continuing to die and crumble. There was nothing left to hold my arm in place.

Surgery was set for October 23rd, and the pain grew to a point beyond any I had ever experienced. I could not walk or stand unassisted, I was using diapers, and I was in a state beyond agony. The enemy was there too.

At one point, my tiny, younger sister was helping me in the bathroom. I was in so much pain, I could not humanly handle it. I was crying and cursing Satan, defying him, insulting him, daring him to take my life. I slung every verbal insult imaginable at him, defying him to take my body. I even offered him my soul. He would have to take me "as is," knowing that even in the very pit of hell, I would be singing praises to my Lord and Savior, Jesus Christ. So, unless he wanted to hear an eternity of praise songs to God, he might as well back off.

The physicians were able to do my surgery early—October 2nd, my fifty-third birthday. Truly answered prayer.

During the administration of anesthesia, I woke up but could not move or talk. I could only listen as the resident rammed an IV into my neck, an area he was told not to mess with because of my brain stimulators behind the arteries. I could only lie there as I felt the blood roll down the back of my neck. I heard them talking about a chief resident being fired because the woman she was working on "bled out and died."

The last thing I heard was that my blood pressure was dropping really fast. I remember thinking, "Well, I guess I am going to get to see Jesus on my birthday." I woke up in recovery, and I am still here.

I am doing great and have received blessings from so many. I have a long way to go in my recovery, but I know I am never alone. Renting a moving van to bring stuff home tomorrow.

What I have learned is that there is never an easy way out, but once we get through the muck and the mire, oh, what a blessed day awaits us!

To those who prayed for me, I thank you with all of my heart. Those of you who took Gidget for walks and picked up her poo-poo will surely be rewarded in heaven. To those who sent balloons, flowers, and cards, you made me smile. I thank you. Those who visited me blessed me more than you will ever know. Those who sent chocolate are numbered with the saints.

Trust God

"Consider it pure joy, my brothers and sisters, whenever you face trials of many kinds, because you know that the testing of your faith produces perseverance. Let perseverance finish its work so that you may be mature and complete, not lacking anything" (James 1:2–5).

Since writing this, I have fallen over thirty times, and I've damaged both knees and broken four ribs. Friends ask how I'm doing, and I tell them, "I'm still here, and I'm vertical."

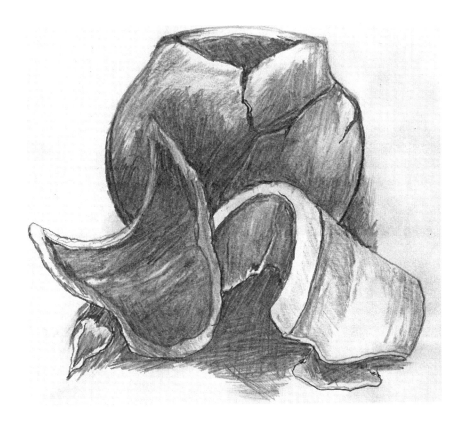

Drawing on His Promises

June 6, 2009

Between seven and ten years ago, my Parkinson's began robbing me of my ability to draw. I have not been able to control my movements enough to draw in over six years.

God is a God who knows our heart's desire. He is a God of restoration.

I have had seven surgeries between 2006 and 2008, including my brain surgeries and a complete shoulder replacement.

My heart's desire is to glorify God and give purpose to my life. In 2006 I began writing and compiling my book of devotions. In 2007 I made and gave away over eight hundred sparrow pins in hopes of blessing others as I have been blessed. In 2008 I made five hundred quilted blankets, most of which were given away or sold to support those in need.

For over seventeen years, I have lived with Parkinson's disease. For three years, I have peered into the pits of hell through the eyes of pain, and through God's graces, I have been lifted to the very pinnacles of glory.

I have gone and continue to go toe-to-toe with the devil. He attacks up-close and personal and fights dirty. I ask only that God use me, flesh and bone, until I am called home.

God is good and has given me purpose and the strength to endure. On Mother's Day of 2009, a small voice urged me to try to draw a friend. I found I could indeed draw again. I can't legibly write a grocery list or write a check, but I can draw portraits.

I stand today—as every day—literally drawing on his promises, loving him, hoping only to glorify him.

In a year I have drawn over 420 portraits and raised about $3,000 for charities. The Bible is filled with God's promises to us. I adore this promise:

"Come to me, all who are weary and burdened, and I will give you rest. Take my yoke upon you and learn from me, for I am gentle and humble in heart, and you will find rest for your souls" (Matt. 11: 28–29).

Open your Bible right now to any page. Put your finger on a verse, and make this verse your devotion for today. It is your promise from God.

Some of my favorite sketches, 400 + faces sketched in one year. To God be the Glory!

Chapter Two
Seek Joy! Introduction

"A cheerful heart is good medicine, but a crushed spirit dries up the bones" (Prov. 17:22).

"Be exalted, O God, above the heavens, and let your glory be over all the earth" (Ps. 108:5).

Joy is an active pursuit. I am convinced that the happier I am in difficult circumstances, the more it ticks Satan off. The more I sing praises to God, the more the enemy throws at me.

No matter what happens, I choose laughter and joy. I choose to praise God with my last breath on this earth and my first breath in glory.

Joy is not easily obtained, nor is it easily held. Joy is peace and light in a world of darkness. I find joy by embracing the child within. Play with a child. Share God with a child. Laugh with a child.

One of the best memories of the past few years came while swinging on a swing set in the park. I had a broken shoulder, brain implants, and acute Parkinson's disease—and I had fun.

I find joy in my art when I push myself beyond limits. I know it was by God's hand that I achieved success. I do not weep for the losses. Instead, I choose to celebrate the God who lifted me beyond my sorrows and sin into joy and life everlasting. To God be the glory; great things he has done!

My best hint for finding joy is to climb out of yourself and bless someone else. Remember:

"A cheerful heart is good medicine, but a crushed spirit dries up the bones" (Prov. 17:22).

Strawberries n' Cream – oil painting, circa 1972

The defining nature of a progressive, degenerative disease is loss of self. So much has been lost, redefined, and/or compromised—my ability to speak as a motivational speaker, to teach, to paint, to play. Yet God continues to encourage me. I am so very blessed by my rediscovered gift of writing. I thank you for encouraging me by reading these pages.

As these pages fade, I stand in defiance of my disease, shouting, "By God's grace, I'm still here!" I will not go gently into that good night. As I boldly battle this beast, this disease, I consider my God. His love is ever present, his strength is ever growing, and I cling to his abiding grace and peace daily.

May my life and praises be as sweet to God's tongue as cool cream and sweet berries.

If

by Karen Petty, age seventeen
1972

If I have only one life,
Let it be spent joyfully and
With a small amount of concern.

If I have only one love
Let it be strong and full of compassion.
For ... yet is it not love, that makes a life?

If I have only one death,
Let my passing be as a test
for those who follow ...

If I have only one soul,
Let it be swept from my body and
Sent upon heaven's threshold.

For ... Yet, is it not my soul
that holds the key to
everlasting life, love, and death.

Seek Joy

"Therefore we do not lose heart. Though outwardly we are wasting away, yet inwardly we are being renewed day by day. For our light and momentary troubles are achieving for us an eternal glory that far outweighs them all. So we fix our eyes not on what is seen, but on what is unseen, since what is seen is temporary, but what is unseen is eternal" (2 Cor. 4:16–18).

Christ is my joy. He is my strength. He is my song.

"The Lord is my strength and my shield; my heart trusts in him, and he helps me. My heart leaps for joy, and with my song I praise him" (Ps. 28:7).

Here is the same poem, revised after becoming a little more mature in my faith—thirty-five years more mature, but who's counting? Since the first writing, I have graduated summa cum laude from the School of Hard Knocks, where the class yell is *"Ow!"*

If

Revised, November 2010

If I have one life only
May I live it with joy.

If I have only one love,
let it be as Christ's love
full of power and compassion.
May that love define my life.

If I have but one death,
Let my passing from this world,
be an example of hope fulfilled
for those who follow.

If I have only one soul,
May it leave my body gently, swiftly
And eternally rest,
breathing in the bounties that await …

Dog Spelled Backwards

Dog spelled backwards is *God*; we've all heard this. If we look at our dogs and their love for us, we can see lessons in how we should regard our God.

Everything I learned about parenting, trust, and unconditional love, I learned from my pets. I've had pet pigs, flying squirrels, chipmunks, dogs, cats, pigeons, and a monkey. I was a talented dog trainer. The following excerpt is from my book, *How to Train a More Godly Dog.* Training animals has given me a richer insight into my relationship with God.

Trying to be human is hard work for our pups.

First, they employ English as a second language. Then, we do everything contrary to their wishes. Just when they get to smelling good, we give them a bath. Just when the trash is ripe for the picking, we throw it out.

We insist that they poop outside, and then we pick it up and carry it back into the house to throw it away. To test the limits of their love for us, we go potty in their favorite water bowl, the toilet. With all we do wrong, they still love us, and their greatest desire is to be with us.

What a wonderful reflection of God's desire for fellowship with us. Does God wag his tail when we call his name? Do you wag your tail when he calls you to serve him, or do you piddle on the carpets and make excuses? The most important rule is this: Don't give up on the pup!

When we sin and disobey God, when we forget the rules and chew on God's favorite slippers or pee on his new carpet, you don't see him dragging us back to the pound and exclaiming, "This just isn't working out for me. Can I try another breed of human—maybe something smaller with less hair?"

Smile! God loves you!

God delights in you. Do you delight in him?

"He brought me out into a spacious place, he rescued me" (2 Sam. 22:20).

Seek Joy!

What is the one thing you love most about people, animals, a loved one, or a friend?

Today, ponder the positive, and know that God is there.

Carolyn's Tony – pencil sketch, 2010

When Love Abides

June 2006

A collar removed, farewell,
thank you,
a loving charge, go on …

An empty collar rests,
lonely reminder of boundless love,
not measured by degree,
bidding me remember, play,
and love abundantly.

A collar removed,
a loving farewell,
thank you for loving me.

A loving charge,
go on, dear friend,
and play eternally.
I will e'er remember you,
will you remember me?

An empty collar,
a ball dropped at my feet,
a challenge from a friend,
love again,
that one may teach you more than me.

When love abides
in willing hearts, who dare to love again,
and born anew, this gift so true,
from God to all who see
the circle never-ending of love eternally.

And when I meet my Savior,
behind Him I will see,
another symbol of his love,
running joyfully to me.

Down the Road, Up the Hill – 1988

In 1968 I was thirteen years old. My family lived deep in the woods and high on a hill. The walk up the hill was about a mile. We typically walked that distance at least twice a day, going to and from our school bus stop.

In the spring, I loved walking down my road, up my hill. The trees were brilliant green, and the wildflowers bloomed everywhere you looked. The brook at the bottom of the hill was cool and clear and always had an abundance of minnows and crawfish. In the summer, I would walk to get the mail. I loved walking barefoot over the cool, smooth stones in the brook.

Sometimes on brisk fall mornings I would see deer grazing on tufts of grass peeking out of the leaves that covered the ground.

Spring, summer, and fall offered many wonderful sights down my road up the hill, but winter was my favorite season. One wintry day while I was walking alone, the trees were covered with snow, and the snow beneath my feet left a familiar crunching sound echoing in the air.

The sky was gray. The trees were bare, with their dark branches reaching into the cold wintry air like fingers, as if they had been drawn onto the sky with ebony ink on brilliant white paper.

I stood watching my breath make clouds in the morning air. The only sounds were the snow crunching under my boots and the pounding of my heart. When a huge shadow moved across the road behind me, I stood motionless as the it passed over me.

It was a mature, fully grown snow owl with a wingspan that stretched the full width of the road. Its beautiful, white, speckled underbelly soared no more than four feet over my head. It flew silently along the snowy path. As I watched this exquisite creature soar away, my heart pounded in rhythm with the slow upturning of each wing. I knew I had been blessed. I had witnessed a creature of such beauty that very few people will ever see.

Most of my winter memories of my road up the hill were of sledding down the road with my brothers and sister. The road was never plowed, so all winter the snow and ice stayed in the ruts and made a snow and ice pack that could stand up to the best ski slope. We would sled down the road up the hill on anything we could find. One winter we took the hood off of an old farm truck, and the four of us had a glorious time—until Dad got home and took one look at his truck. I did most of my sledding with my red wooden sled. As I glided swiftly down the hill, my body moved as if one with the sled, turning and bounding with each bump and rut in the road. The cold, crisp air nipped at our faces and fingertips, and we did not seem to notice the cold as much as we do today.

There were many bad things that happened to me in my childhood, but I thank God that I can focus on the positive and joyful gifts from God, like sledding down my road, up the hill.

Seek Joy

"How abundant are the good things that you have stored up for those who fear you, that you bestow in the sight of all on those who take refuge in you" (Ps. 31:19).

What is your favorite memory from your childhood? Share it with a young person. I guarantee they will enjoy it and you.

Morning Mist – watercolor, circa 1978

My Horse, Paint

Paint had beautiful blue eyes. Paint was a black-and-white, painted quarter horse. He ate pork and beans and slept under the pear tree outside my bedroom window. In the summer, Paint liked it when my sister and I kept the bedroom window open. He would whinny and snort as we laughed and played. When the pears fell from the trees, Paint would eat them. He made slurpy sounds as he greedily devoured each pear. Unfortunately, pears gave Paint gas. We slept with the window closed a lot.

If God ever allows animals in heaven, I hope to see Paint again. He suffered neglect, abuse, and nutritional hardships like the rest of my family. He taught us all about unconditional love. His barn was drafty and cold. His food was substandard. He was a great companion and teacher.

My father sold him the fall of my junior year of high school. I still miss him and dream about him. I hope he was sold to a good family. I hope we meet again. In a very dreary childhood, Paint brought us joy and happy memories.

"Ask the beasts and they will tell you, they will teach you ... In His hands is the life of every living thing, and the breath of all mankind" (Job 12:7–10).

Seek Joy

Through Paint, I learned to love unconditionally and to
play—and even to laugh in difficult circumstances.

Each day, each moment, is indeed sacred. Joy is a choice. It must be actively
pursued Too often we hold our bitterness and sadness as a banner. They
become part of us. If we are to know true joy, we must cast off the bonds
of bitterness.

I suggest that you put this book aside for a while and go play. Do chalk
drawings on your street or sidewalk, blow bubbles, make snow angels. The
chalk drawings will cheer your neighbors and can be a way to share the
gospel. Play with the joy of the Lord in your heart.

It is in his joy that we find peace. It is in his joy that we find the strength
to move beyond our circumstances and bless others. God is waiting.

Now go, play, laugh with God. Play on a swing, blow bubbles, or blow
bubbles while swinging. Go!

The Lesson – reproduction, Thomas Hart Benton, seventh grade

Without Ceasing

What a glorious, wonderful, awesome God! He set the very cosmos in motion and still he loves, weeps for, and delights in me.

Seek Joy

"The Lord your God is with you, he is mighty to save. He will take great delight in you, he will quiet you with his love, he will rejoice over you with singing" (Zeph. 3:17).

God delights in you. His desire is relationship, fellowship with you. Pray at least five times today. Allow God to nurture you through time spent in prayer and praise.

God delights in you and me!
Our amazing God delights in us

Without Ceasing

Oh, Lord, my God, how tender is the morning,
You lift my head that I might see the day.
Oh, Lord, my God, how firm is my foundation.
You give me hope to wonder at the heavens
And wisdom now to humbly bow and pray.

Oh, Lord, my God, how radiant the midday sun,
Brightly burn your strength in me,
As faith's bright embers light my way
In grace and peace abiding, Lord,
Stand with me all the day.

Oh, Lord, my God, the day was long, and I'm so weary,
Yet, oh, my God, how glorious the setting sun,
How soft the pillow of my prayers,
placed gently 'neath my head,
My prayers you hear and hold upon your heart
Till dawn breaks through and we begin anew.

Service Dog Gidget — acrylic on canvas
Trained by C.H.A.M.P. Assistance Dogs Inc.
St. Louis, Missouri

Into the Eyes of Love

In 1999 I applied to CHAMP Assistance Dogs for a service dog. My Parkinson's disease was advancing quickly. I was told that they would place a public access service dog with me within a year. In 1999 a pup named Gidget came into their program. She was a high-steppin' ball of fluff and energy, and I fell head-over-heals in love. I watched her grow, always from a distance. I knew she was too young to ever be my dog, and to pet her would have been sheer torture for me. I remember telling my husband that I needed prayer; I knew I would love whatever dog they gave me, but I also knew I would hate whoever got Gidget.

Three years passed, and I finally got my service dog. It was Gidget. I have never known a more devoted friend than my Gidge. When I am in the hospital, she sleeps in front of the door at home, awaiting my return.

On two occasions when I was in the hospital for over a month, she was allowed to stay with me. She slept at my feet and would get a nurse when I needed help.

Friends and church members would take her outside several times a day. If they were new to the job, Gidget would guide them safely through the winding hospital corridors to the park outside. When she was ready, she would swiftly guide them back to my room. When I am in a lot of pain, she refuses to leave my side for any reason.

She has been my shield for over eight years. No one sees me or my disability, they see only her love for me and her beauty. I have often said that if I were ever to rob a bank, witnesses would describe me as a short blonde lady with wavy hair, big brown eyes, and a big black nose.

The other day, her vet called her a geriatric. She may be graying in the face, but with that gray comes the confidence and assurance of a pro. She is good at what she does. She is an assistance dog and she is love.

All you have to do is look into her eyes. Every moment of the day I am blessed with the privilege of looking into the eyes of love. She opens more than doors for me; she opens people's hearts. We have a bond of interdependence that is stronger than I had ever dreamed.

On a lighter note: People occasionally confuse her with guide dogs. When I would get out of the driver's seat of the car wearing my sunglasses, people would sometimes express concerns over my ability to drive. I just tell them she barks once for right and twice for left, and off we go. Oddly enough, they are okay with that.

Seek Joy

Sometimes joy is easily obtained. If you are lucky, joy will walk right up and lick you in the face.

"Every good and perfect gift is from above, coming down from the Father of the heavenly lights, who does not change like shifting shadows" (James 1:17).

List twenty good and perfect gifts from God.
Now thank him for each individual gift.

Clearly I have too much time on my hands.

Joy like beauty is in the eye of the beholder.

Gone Fishin' – pencil sketch

Gone Fishin'

Yesterday my husband and I impulsively left on a spur-of-the-moment fishing trip—something we had not done in about thirty years. I'd had surgery on Wednesday, and on Saturday we were on our way to Montauk State Park. He was lamenting missing the last day of trout season. I said he should go, and he said he couldn't because of my surgery. I said, "Go!" He said, "We can't." I said, "Let's go!" And we went.

There are few things of such natural beauty as my husband and a river in the early fall. The morning mist hangs heavily over the water as we wait for the morning bell that signals the last day of trout season. He stands up to his chest in waders and water. My goodness, its cold. My hands and fingers are frozen to the bone. He seems impervious to the cold.

The bell sounds, and the line sings as he throws it in its guided path. He deftly places the line halfway across the river and a little upstream.

He hands the rod to me. My arm has been badly injured by a fall three years earlier. I can't cast or land a fish alone, but he is there to help. "Now, let it set there awhile," he counsels. Soon I feel the wonder, the anticipation of fishing, and the rod tip gently bends, suggesting the interest of a passing trout. "Wait for it," he cautions, "let him take it, wait, wait ..." Then he advises, "Now, reel him in," which I have been trying to do since I felt the first nibble on my line.

As I reel in the first catch of the day, he advises, "Keep your line tight. Now bring him over to the bank. Smooth." My heart pounds as he pulls my fish from the icy water. "Big enough to keep, good eatin' size," he adds, and my heart quickens as I begin my marathon of emotions.

First, I feel pride in landing such a big, little fish. Then, I feel remorse as I consider a life ended by me. I quickly consider my options—release it or keep it—as the beautiful rainbow trout flops around, literally a fish out of water. And before I know it, I have given the fish a death sentence. The disposal method of choice is to soak it in sea salt brine and slowly smoke it over a grill for about three hours. It will be tasty on crackers with sun-dried tomato pesto.

My attention is again focused on the beauty of the river, the waterfall, and my husband. He is more interested in my catching a fish than in his own empty stringer. He does his fishing later in the day, when everyone else has given up for the day.

I witness him patiently throwing his line time and again across the water, hearing the familiar whisper of the line as it cuts through the crisp morning air. I feel the vapor as the line flies back again to spank the air in an audible pop as the line now flies forward again. He and the line seeming more fluid than the river itself.

Memory carries me back more than thirty-five years to a brisk March morning with about five inches of snow on the ground, when I was introduced to trout fishing. My future husband was advising me to dip my rod tip in the water to clear the line of ice.

"But this water is fr-fr-freezing," I told him, having firsthand knowledge from my fall into the icy brink only moments before.

"It'll work," he assured me.

"Okay," I stuttered, too frozen to argue. Then humiliation added to humiliation, and I slipped and fell in again. He grabbed my shirt collar and snatched me out of the freezing water.

"The other fishermen don't like it when the water gets muddy, ya know." My lips were blue, as were every finger and toe. My husband still recalls my lips and the fact that I looked like a half-drowned kitten. Then he suggested that we might want to go in and warm up a bit.

I thought then how great God was, and how beautiful the world was. I fell in love with trout fishing and deeper in love with my boyfriend. I remember wishing I could paint a picture. I still haven't painted a picture as beautiful or as immediate as those moments.

I think God gives us experiences and memories that are too immediate, too glorious for words. Neither camera nor artist's canvas could capture such an image. It's a glimpse of the glory that awaits us.

Seek Joy

"For the director of music. A psalm of David. The heavens declare the glory of God; the skies proclaim the work of his hands" (Ps. 19:1).

Have you experienced the immediate beauty of God's creation? Try to describe the experience and your feelings.

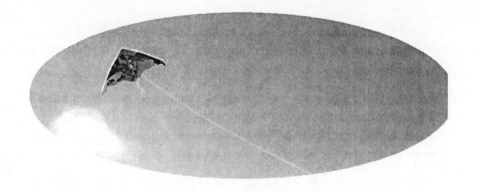

Go Fly a Kite

September 2, 2007

Oh, but that we were more like the kite
Than the person holding it to the earth.
A kite struggles and battles to soar free.
It was made to seek the heavens.

A kite soars and tugs at the string
that holds it to the earth.
It will battle wind, rain, and gravity to fly.
How hard do we fight to be closer to God?

A kite knows it's single purpose—to fly.
Do we know our single, God-given purpose—
To love and be loved by Him?
To carry and witness always of God's love?

As I lose my physical abilities
to speak, to teach, to play,
I consider that simple God-given purpose.
As spring approaches,
Go fly a kite!

Consider God's strength,
His abiding love,
Our purpose …
And
As the kite strains at the string
That holds it to the earth,
Consider
What awaits us
When
We break free!

Seek Joy

"Jesus answered him, 'I tell you the truth, today you will be with me in paradise'" (Luke 23:43).

Today take at least ten minutes to look at the sky and soak in God's love for you. Climb into his lap and breathe him in. Close your eyes and feel his embrace, warm and safe.

Oh, my glorious God, I do love you. My heart races when I think about you. How lovely you are, my good and lovely God.

What would you whisper in God's ear today?
What song would you write for God?
How could you share his glory with someone else?
Go, do it.

Chapter Three
Live Boldly Introduction

A life lived boldly is a life lived to its fullest, with few regrets and even fewer apologies. How does one live such a life? With God by your side, a life lived boldly is very possible. Few regrets do not mean one is perfectly satisfied with his life. I am far from satisfied. I am always asking God to give my life purpose. When given a godly purpose, I cannot help but boldly jump in to get things done. When my God is directing moves, there is a confidence and assurance that comes with each life experience.

To live a life with few apologies means simply that I have endeavored to harm no one with action or words. I do apologize for the wrongs I've done, and I apologize to God for my human frailties and grief for which I alone am responsible.

A life lived boldly is comprised of risk, the possibility of failure, and tremendous joy in success. The cornerstone of a life lived boldly is communication—with and honoring of a holy, righteous God.

Read this passage from Hebrews 11:1–7.

"Now faith is being sure of what we hope for and certain of what we do not see. This is what the ancients were commended for. By faith we understand that the universe was formed at God's command, so that what is seen was not made out of what was visible.

"By faith Abel offered God a better sacrifice than Cain did. By faith he was commended as a righteous man when God spoke well of his offerings. And by faith he still speaks, even though he is dead.

"By faith Enoch was taken from this life … And without faith it is impossible to please God, because anyone who comes to him must believe that he exists and that he rewards those who earnestly seek him.

"By faith Noah, when warned about things not yet seen, in holy fear build an ark to save his family" (Heb. 11:1–7).

The Rain Tree

In the evening when the night air blew through my window, I would sit and wonder what mountains it had touched, whose hair it had caressed, and what dreams were carried on its wings.

Today I wonder, "Who am I?" Where is the person who used to delight in the simplest of pleasures: a falling leaf caught dancing in the wind, a squirrel at play, a glorious sunset, or the blackened sky filled with a billion shimmering eyes?

I try to recall those moments that I cherished, but most of them are shaded with sadness. The memory of a loving brother's eyes haunts me—young voices at play, my calling, "Wes, wait for me" and hearing, "Come on, hurry up, Sis,"—all the while knowing that Death had swallowed him into her silent world.

The beauty and the cherished memories of my place of peace, my place of contentment, shall never be tarnished. In the outrage and shame that sent me running, I knew that eventually there would be peace. And there was always hope.

As I try to recall my peaceful place, my most vivid memories are of the crackling leaves as I ran to get there. Along with my anger and shame, bursting through the silent woods, there was also my glory in seeing the solitude—the majesty—of my tree. It stood tall with its tender blanket of cool moss, spread wide to envelope me. Beneath the tree was a hollowed piece of the mountain, not quite a cave, but always sheltering from the rain or cool winds.

In the spring, the tree would erupt with promise, buds of hope and beauty. Beneath the tree's branches, its trunk stood in the midst of a bed of sweet moss with roses that opened in the morning to greet me and closed in the evening, keeping secret their treasures in the silent moonlight.

The tree itself overwhelmed me with its size and quiet strength. Several times I thought of climbing its branches to try to see the world from the top through its eyes, but I would not dare to steal its secrets, its visions. I sat, contented to be cradled by its branches; there I knew I would be safe.

The sounds came flooding back: the wind softly combing through the leaves; the squirrels rustling about, dodging imaginary foes in their games through fallen leaves; the calming rhythm of water passing over rocks in the stream nearby; the birds, each with its own separate melody of peace; the smell of crisp leaves, of cool moss, of a fallen tree, of the brook … In all these there is a magic, a peace.

I remember one particular day with my tree and my solitude. I collapsed at the base of my tree, the coolness caressing my face—red, hot, and beaten. After the tears, after the pounding of my heart had grown silent, I sat up, my arms cradling my tired, defeated body, and I gazed down at the rocks below. The wind was silent, and I wondered if the world would ever be right for me. Then from a distance I heard it, a sound that I will never forget and that I have never heard since: a faint whirring, a powerful sound growing louder with each beat of my heart.

I looked up to see, hovering so close that I could touch it, a gentle hummingbird. It stayed only for a moment as my senses drank in its beauty: the vibrant green, its delicate wings, its slender bill, and the sparkle of life in its eyes. Then it was gone, leaving only an echo of its wings as they stirred the wind and the wondrous feast of my senses.

When I remember my place, its shelter, its peace, I recall the lines from my favorite movie, *Raintree County*: "We Americans measure greatness in simple terms, in terms of money. We are always searching for the "tree of life," whose fruit is pure gold; but there is another tree, not of gold, but of fulfillment, whose flower is accomplishment and whose fruit is love, whose ways are the ways of pleasantness and whose paths all lead to peace."

Live Boldly

A life lived boldly is one in which hope and love flourish beyond earthly circumstances. God truly desires the best for us. I know and have witnessed time and again his unfailing love. In considering my life's circumstances, I know that all of the bad things, all of my suffering, have not been in vain. God has, does, and will continue to use me however he chooses. Sometimes I get angry with God because I am scared or in pain, or I am discontented with my illness, wishing I could be healthy for my family.

I have railed against God on numerous occasions. He loves me still and tenderly carries me back to my place of fulfillment. He has been and ever shall be my comfort and my strength.

We all have issues with God because of his very nature. He accepts our issues, though most should rightfully be thrown in Satan's face. If you could dump one burden, one heartache, one pain right back in Satan's face, what would it be?

Describe your place of fulfillment.

"The Lord is my strength and my song; He has become my salvation. He is my God and I will praise Him, my Father's God and I will exalt Him" (Ex. 15:2).

This is a photo of me at eighteen, shortly before leaving home. Our family pet, Wolf, stands beside me.

The Gift

This photo was taken on my eighteenth birthday, about eight days before I left home. In retrospect, my leaving home was truly a leap of faith.

I did the painting in this chair when I was seventeen. I remember being beaten for doing this painting. I was accused of feeling too good for the rest of the family. The painting was damaged when it was thrown at me. The oil paint was still wet, and I thought the painting was ruined. I was able to repair the painting, but not my broken heart. I began using drugs. I see now that I was forcing myself to an emotional cliff. Either jump and allow myself to be consumed by drugs and alcohol, or turn around and choose life. I chose life.

On October 10, 1973, eight days after my eighteenth birthday, I left home. I didn't know where I was going to sleep from one day to the next. I was still in high school and hiding from my dad, who threatened to burn the house of anyone who helped me. Even in my leaving home, God was guiding me. I met my future husband. He was a youth counselor at a house for runaways where I stayed for about two months.

After leaving Youth Emergency Services, I lived with different people, including the assistant principal of my high school. Up until this point in my life, nearly everyone I met had tried to hurt me. I was learning to trust.

In November of 1973, I met Mom Simpson, my foster mom, and found a family who taught me to love and trust. The following story is about my foster mom, Doris Janet Meadows Simpson, to whom I gave this painting.

There lives in some of us an inextinguishable spark, a beauty that shines through in all circumstances. That is what I remember most about Mom's smile. When I first met her, I was eighteen years old and needed a home. She was tall and strong, so patient and quiet. I could see the love in her laughing eyes. I didn't know at the time how deeply Mom Simpson would affect my life.

At the time, my only concern was finding a place to live. When her husband, my eighth grade science teacher, asked if she wanted to "give it a try," she turned to me, smiled lovingly, and asked, "Well, Karen, do you want to give *us* a try?" I looked at that sofa with Mom, Dad, and their three children, all sitting together, reaching out as a family. "Yes," I said quietly.

Coming from a lifetime of physical, verbal, and sexual abuse, this too was a leap of faith. God used the Simpson family to teach me to trust. I had found a home. I lived with my new family a little more than a year. During that time, Mom taught me to cook, clean, sew, and—most of all—to love, trust, and laugh. All these things she taught me with strength, love, and a smile. During the short time I lived with them, Dad was always challenging me with questions, philosophies, and ethics.

It was Mom to whom I looked for comfort and guidance. I watched her rush around the house, cleaning, cooking, and teaching. She taught fourth grade and always had time for me and her children. I never heard a harsh word from her, nor a sigh of fatigue. Even after working all day, she would drive little Shelly to dance lessons or the boys to ball games. Hers was truly a sacrificial, unconditional love. Her life was a smile generated from deep within her heart.

I eventually moved away, first to an apartment nearby, and then to college. I carried with me the memory of her smile, larger than life itself. The years passed, and I married my husband Mike. We had a daughter of our own. I learned that Mom had rheumatoid arthritis. I didn't know what horrors that disease would bring to her.

Months went by, and Mom became more and more frail. Her pain showed in her posture, her eyes, even in her voice; but her smile was enduring. As she grew more frail with each passing month, I realized that this disease would take her from us.

As with many tragedies, there were tender moments. One such tender moment was the first time Mom held my daughter. She held her tightly, whispered to her as she looked in her eyes, then looked up at me and smiled.

Months passed, and mom was placed on a respirator. She grew weaker with each passing day. She was losing her battle with this disease. All of her courage, strength, and love could not save her. In retrospect, I see ironically that it was that same courage, strength, and love that saved *me*.

The last time I saw Mom, she was in a hospital bed. We were alone, and I was holding her hands. They were getting cold and blue. Life was running from her. I remember not wanting to leave her, hoping I could generate some warmth into her hands if I could keep holding them. But I had to leave, and as I turned to go, Mom woke up. "I love you," I said. "I'll see you tomorrow." She looked at me and smiled.

The next morning, Dad called and told me that she was gone. I cried because her suffering was over and she was in heaven. Most of all I cried out of gratitude for having known and loved such a beautiful person, one who had loved me so completely and unconditionally, who had so tenderly presented to me one last precious gift … her smile.

"So we say with confidence, 'The Lord is my helper; I will not be afraid.
What can man do to me?'"
(Heb. 13:6).

Live Boldly

How has God shown his abiding love for you? My bold life choices are based on my trust in God and his love for me. What can you trust God for today? How does it feel to give this burden to God?

In the 1970s a popular phrase was, "God is dead." This was my response to that statement.

God Lives

November 25, 1972

God lives in the sparrow of springtime,
In the essence and beauty of summer and fall,
and in the white flowing blanket of winter.

God lives in the eyes and heart of a newborn baby,
in the whisper of a summer night's wind,
and the petals of an unfolding bud.

God lives in my every thought,
in every moment of joy,
and also those of sorrow.

In the course of my lifetime,
there has been no greater pleasure,
nor anything so dear to my heart,
than that of knowing
that God lives!

"How great are His signs, how mighty His wonders! His kingdom is an eternal kingdom, His dominion endures from generation to generation" (Dan. 4:3).

Today, praise God for creation and salvation.

God Lives

Revised, October 17, 2007

God lives in the sparrow of springtime,
in the whisper of a summer night's wind,
in the essence and beauty of fall,
in the soft flowing blanket of winter,
God lives!
He lives in them all!

God lives in the eyes of a baby,
in the promise of an unfolding bud,
in the heart and hands of a stranger,
reaching out in service and love,
God lives!
He lives in them all!

God lives in all that surrounds us,
in every beat of my heart,
in each breathless moment of turning
from sorrow toward joy and contentment,
Rising up to God's love sublime,
God lives!
He lives in my heart!

In the course of my lifetime,
no greater pleasure I've known,
nothing so dear to my heart,
Than knowledge and truth everlasting,
God lives! He lives in us all!

Angels Among Us

There are events in our lives that, as they are unfolding, seem commonplace to us. It is not until the picture is fully revealed that we see the comedy—the miracle of it all.

This story began months earlier with a trip to a local auto repair shop. I had taken my car in to have a loose emergency brake release cable repaired. The repair had supposedly been done. I paid the repair charge, and the comedy of errors began.

The repair had not been done properly. On subsequent visits to the dealership, I brought this to his attention. He assured me that it was fixed. "It works, don't it, Ma'am? Then it's fixed," was his reply.

"But the cable release is still loose," I told him.

"Can't fix what ain't broken," he assured me.

On one visit I was told, "Why, you don't really even need that cable. If it breaks, just pull that little piece of metal under the dash. Then come in the next day and speak to the shop manager.

That evening I went to work, and on my way home I stopped to pick up a few things for my daughter's sixteenth birthday party. I pulled into the parking lot of the Maplewood Venture Store. I am disabled with a degenerative neuromuscular disease. I always try to be courteous when using handicapped parking, so I parked in the space farthest from the store, leaving the closer spaces open for those who may have been more disabled than I was. This is also for the convenience of those healthy people who park illegally and run into the stores, totally oblivious of their own selfishness. (I digress and should get back to the story.)

After I finished shopping and returned to my car, I started it, put it in reverse, and noticed that the parking brake was on. I pulled the release cable. It was really loose now, and it broke off in my hand. I was tired, frustrated, and just wanted to go home. I remembered the words of my trusted mechanic, "Just pull on this little metal thing, and it will release the brake." Boy, I wish I had paid attention to which little metal piece he was talking about.

I searched and searched for that little metal thing. It was dark, and I couldn't see over the dash very well, so I decided to get out of my car to get a better look. Because of my disability, I can't bend or stoop very well, so I sat on the pavement next to the car. With the door open, I began searching under the dash for "that little metal thing." I finally found it.

I thought I was a mechanic. My car thought I was a speed bump. In my fatigue and frustration, I had forgotten that my car was still running … and in reverse.

When I pulled "that little metal thing," the car shot back, immediately pinning my right foot between the tire and the pavement. I watched the car as it rolled up my right ankle, turned my calf sideways, and proceeded up my leg toward my knee. At this point, I thought, "Man, this is really gonna hurt tomorrow!"

I screamed for help and tried to warn others who might be in the path of my rogue car. I continued to watch as my car made its way along its path to my thigh. I thought I should lie down and let the car door pass over me to avoid being dragged by the tires. I tried to roll my torso as far from the wheels as possible. I tried desperately to remain in control. I was not in control.

God was in control. I watched as my car rolled up my thigh and over my hip. At some point, the car turned and the passenger side tires rolled over both legs, pulling me under the car. This is where it really gets good.

As if possessed, my car backed neatly into the closest parking space. Someone jumped in, turned the car off, and put on the parking brake. Maplewood's finest were quickly on the scene. I was laughing and crying at the same time. I cried because of the pain and laughed because of the foolishness.

The officer urgently asked, "Who ran over you, Lady?'

I answered, "Well, I kinda did."

He looked down at me, stepped back, and asked, "You ran over yourself?"

"Well, it was a lot easier than it sounds," I said.

Needing more details, he asked, "Where did this happen?"

Lying there on the hot pavement, tire tracks all over my legs and my arm twisted behind me, suddenly I did not feel like the only fool in that parking lot. "Well, pretty much right here, Sir," I told him.

The ambulance arrived and things got more chaotic. There were so many wonderful people who came to my aid that evening. There were more cell phones than I had ever seen outside of a Radio Shack. People came with first aid kits, blankets, and ice packs.

One woman came with prayer. She was middle-aged, black, wore glasses, spoke with a gentle voice, and had the softest hands. She held my hand and asked if we could pray. "Yes," I said, "please pray with me." I was distracted, and as the paramedics and police did their jobs, she prayed. She drew close to me, looked calmly into my eyes and said, "You are not going to be harmed by this."

She leaned even closer to me, looked firmly into my eyes and said, "You do not understand. You are not going to be harmed by this. Do you believe me?" I looked into her soft, calm, brown eyes, held her gentle hand, and lied to her. I said, "I believe you."

"Lady," I thought, "I have just run over myself with a Ford Taurus wagon—a fully loaded, automatic-doors-and-windows, factory-built-and-installed air conditioner, very heavy Ford Taurus wagon with a full tank of gas. I hurt already. I may be stupid, but I'm not crazy. You run over yourself with a car, it's gonna hurt!"

The paramedics radioed ahead to Barnes Emergency, using words like "broken hip, contusion, possible spinal injury," and she was telling me that I would not be harmed!

In the ambulance, her assurances echoed in my heart. "Do you believe me?" Her words suddenly became words from God. "Whatever you ask in

My name, I will do it that the Son of Man may bring glory to the Father" (John 14:13).

"Do you believe me?" Her words gave me the confidence to go before the Lord with a boldness that I had never known before. In my Savior's precious name, I commanded that there be no broken bones. Later that night, the doctor, having reviewed my x-rays, came in with astounding news. He couldn't believe it. There were no broken bones. I would be going home. He told me that the last person he'd seen run over by a car didn't go home.

He said I would need intense physical therapy, as there was severe muscular-skeletal damage, and I would be in a lot of pain for some time. He gave me some very strong pain pills and said that if they were not strong enough, to contact my doctor for stronger ones. He told me that I wouldn't be able to walk for several weeks and that I should see my primary care physician the next day.

I didn't need any of the pain pills. I walked with help from my car to the house that night, very slowly, but walking nonetheless. And I received no physical therapy.

I believe that angels walk among us. I do not believe this precious woman was an angel. She looked nothing like Della Reese. I do believe that God uses real people to do the work of angels. I would like to find this earth angel, to thank her, join hands with her, and stand together in praise of our wonderful God. I know that I will find her. If not here, then when we are together in his presence.

Live Boldly

"Do not forget to show hospitality to strangers, for by so doing some people have shown hospitality to angels without knowing it" (Heb. 14:2).

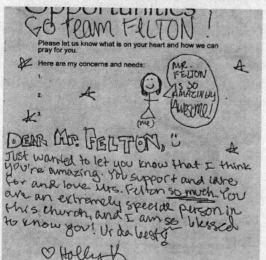

Live Steady

Be strong
infinitely faithful
the journey is long.

We're watching
and learning
not by word
but by deed
you teach us
you lead us.

Your honor
your courage
your faith now we see
infinite, eternal
how God has loved thee.

Live steady
be strong
infinitely faithful
the journey is long.

Live Boldly

"For this very reason, make every effort to add to your faith goodness; and to goodness, knowledge; and to knowledge, self-control; and to self-control, perseverance; and to perseverance, godliness; and to godliness, mutual affection; and to mutual affection, love. For if you possess these qualities in increasing measure, they will keep you from being ineffective and unproductive in your knowledge of our Lord Jesus Christ" (2 Peter 1:5–8).

Letter from Kevin

God Is in Control

March 28, 2009

Once again, God teaches that he is in control. As my feelings of uselessness grow, my pain again controls who and what I am. As even typing is more and more difficult, God teaches me to hang on. Everything, even my loneliness has a purpose. Others are watching and learning about perseverance, faith, and hope—and through our life together, love.

These were copies of letters from former Sunday school students. Two notes were given to my husband and me during worship service. What an encouragement they were.

I so long for heaven. I am in so very much pain. It is getting more difficult to speak. I want my husband to have someone to love and play with while he is still young. I look at the world through the eyes of a ghost these days. I am here, but I'm not here. I have to keep my mind and heart focused on the walk.

It is through the journey that we are made stronger and are perfected. I want to focus more on today and less on heaven.

Time and again, when I am ready to give up, God encourages me through others.

Live Boldly

"Therefore we are always confident and know that as long as we are at home in the body we are away from the Lord. We live by faith, not by sight. We are confident, I say, and would prefer to be away from the body and at home with the Lord" (2 Cor. 5:6–8).

What do you need to focus on these days: heaven or your journey?

Chapter Four
Love Abundantly

Introduction

"And we have seen and testify that the Father has sent his Son to be the Savior of the world. If anyone acknowledges that Jesus is the Son of God, God lives in them and they in God. And so we know and rely on the love God has for us.

"God is love. Whoever lives in love lives in God, and God in him. This is how love is made complete among us so that we will have confidence on the day of judgment: In this world we are like Jesus. There is no fear in love. But perfect love drives out fear, because fear has to do with punishment. The one who fears is not made perfect in love. We love because he first loved us" (1 John 4:14).

The dictionary defines the word abundant as well or richly supplied. The miracle in my life has always been my ability to give and receive love. I have always loved God. It is through Christ and the Holy Spirit that I find earthly love, manifested in my friends.

My husband asked me last night how I could write of God's love and grace when my life has been an unending saga of suffering. He said the only grace he sees is from me. I asked him, "Where do you think my grace comes from?"

I feel God's grace and love surrounding me. Even now as I type this, my pain is so intense and it takes me so long to type or even to move the mouse. It's difficult to keep the focus. I have broken down several times unable to go on. Yet I can do all things through Christ who gives me strength.

My first love song was sung to me by God. My Grammaw and relatives in Imboden, Arkansas, sang love songs to me, and my husband, children, and friends continue in this chorus. I too join to sing to others.

This chorus, if sung in love, continues beyond our days. There is a song in the heart of us all, one whose melody is truth, whose rhythm is written by God, and whose lyrics are composed by those who love us. And our hearts sing it to those we love.

Love is eternal. With God, love lasts forever. With God and his love, we can accomplish great things.

Love Abundantly

"As the Father has loved me, so have I loved you. Now remain in my love. If you obey my commands, you will remain in my love, just as I have obeyed my father's commands and remain in his love. I have told you this so that my joy may be in you and that your joy may be complete.

"My command is this: Love each other as I have loved you. Greater love has no one than this, that he lay down his life for his friends. You are my friends, if you do as I command. I no longer call you servants, because a servant does not know his master's business. Instead, I have called you friends, for everything that I learned from my Father I have made known to you. You did not choose me, but I chose you and appointed you to go and bear fruit that will last. Then the father will give you whatever you ask in my name. This is my command: Love each other" (John 15:9–17).

I Remember Imboden

I remember a quieter time when things moved slower and no one seemed to notice, when front porches were more important than the houses behind them.

I remember a town where the train whistle was as constant and soothing as a sunset.

I remember a moment of hope, when a glass of cold lemonade was offered, accepted, and shared. Slowly we cooled ourselves with soothing drops of water, condensed on our icy glass. I hoped the moment would last forever, but it slipped away as quietly and tenderly as the droplets of water from my glass.

I remember Grammaw's hands, rugged and tender, always holding her Bible as she napped. Her apron smelled of cinnamon and was just the right height for hugging. She was small and mighty with a gentle strength and smiling eyes. Her face was worn by time and worry. Her hair was gray. Her smile was love. She was beautiful.

I remember Grampaw. He was safe and funny and always had the time and inclination to talk. With Grampaw you always knew you were important. He always had the time to talk and a place on his lap. He smelled of wood smoke and chewing tobacco. His eyes were "laughingly" blue. He was wonderful.

95

I remember a brief and quiet place, a moment in time that was created for the young at heart, a place of lemonade summers and ice cream made of snow, a place that makes the memory linger and still takes my breath away. I remember Imboden.

Love Abundantly

"Love is patient, love is kind and envies no one. Love is never boastful, nor conceited, nor rude; never selfish, not quick to take offense. There is nothing love can't face; there is no limit to its faith, its hope, and endurance. In a word, there are three things that last forever: faith, hope and love; but the greatest of these is love" (1 Cor. 13:4–7, 13).

This scripture speaks of love as a living entity. There is nothing that love cannot face. There is no limit to its faith, hope, or endurance. It is ever changing, ever growing.

Where and from whom have you felt true love as God speaks of here?

Who can you share God's living love with?

More Than a House ... Theirs Was a Home

There are places we go in life where we find joy, and we think, *I'd like to come back someday.* There are places we go that a part of us never leaves behind. Grammaw and Grampaw Guthrie's home was that place for me. The house is now gone, and Grammaw and Grampaw have gone to their heavenly home. A part of my heart remains in past moments, cherished and guarded in time.

It is because of these places of gentle laughter and warm memories that we all have a place to go—a home with feather beds, sweet tea, fresh-baked bread, and arms open wide, bidding us come, sit, be loved, rest, and remember.

I remember Grammaw's yard, always abuzz with a flurry of activity and children. We would often pack a lunch and go down to the river. My Grammaw was better at skipping stones across the Arkansas River than anyone around. She easily squeezed six to eight skips from any stone offered her in challenge.

She was so very patient and kind. Grammaw did, however, have her moments and her limits. When pushed beyond all human boundaries, her sense of humor and sense of aim came together in a moment of comedic parenting perfection.

Several kids were running uncontrollably in the yard and jumping the gate, disregarding her numerous explanations of the use and purposes for a gate. After several warnings from Grammaw to stop jumping the fence or "Somebody's gonna get hurt!," she quietly picked up a stone and hurled it over fifty feet across the yard. The stone popped the back of the head of an offending jumper. "Ow!" he yelped, rubbing his head. "That hurt!"

Grammaw quietly reminded them all, "I told you somebody was gonna get hurt." Then she sat back in the porch swing, picked up her Bible, and smiled.

Our lives were pre-television and pre-indoor plumbing. The house was heated with a woodstove. In the winter months, the woodstove always held a pot of coffee and a big pot of beans or homemade soup.

At night, no one slept alone. The feather beds and quilts were always soft and inviting. They smelled like sunshine, because Grammaw always hung her linens on the clothesline, even in the winter months. I remember drinking water from a hand-pump well. It was so cold and sweet, and it made the best glass of lemonade on the planet.

When occupying the outhouse, one had to keep an eye out for rattlesnakes and the occasional bottom-pecking chicken. Life was never boring at Grammaw's.

If we had nothing to do, we enjoyed doing it well.

We lived close to the railroad tracks and could always count on a passing conductor or engineer to wave to us as the train passed by. During my recent trip back there, my sister and I went to the trestle where we played as children. A train passed while we were reminiscing, and the engineer waved as he passed, head and shoulders hanging out of the window, with the broadest smile on his face. We smiled and waved back.

Love Abundantly

"In my father's house are many mansions … I am going there to prepare a place for you" (John 14:2).

The Bible tells me there is a mansion waiting for me. I hope it looks like this. If you could design your mansion, what would it look like?

"The fruit of righteousness is peace, the effect of righteousness is quietness and confidence.
My people will live in peaceful dwelling places, in secure homes, in undisturbed places of rest" (Isa. 32:17–18).

I once read that laziness was nothing more than resting before you get tired, just thought I'd share that with ya.

The Big Fish

This is the smile I will always remember. The smile was inspired by landing a big fish. It is the same smile that I remember every time Grampaw told a story that turned out to be a joke. It was the smile of knowing that he "got" someone—hook, line, and sinker.

Grampaw was a simple man with simple needs: family, friends, and his beloved Gyp—his nickname for Grammaw.

Grammaw was his guiding light, his center, his soul mate, his Big Fish, his reason to smile.

May we all be blessed to be someone's Big Fish, someone's reason to smile.

Love Abundantly

"Many waters cannot quench love; rivers cannot wash it away" (Song 8:7).

Grammaw and Grampaw taught me that true love can last forever. I married a man who is my Big Fish; he makes me smile. I hope that I am still his Big Fish.

I have many friends who light up a room when they come to visit: Janet, Joy, Susana, Terri, Shannon, Annie, Patti, Kathy, Cheryl, Beth, Barb, Diane, and all my students—just to name a few. God is so gracious to have brought these Big Fish into my life.

Make a list of the Big Fish in your life. Copy this little story and share it with them, pray together, and thank God for bringing you together.

The Rose of My Heart

2005

(Dedicated to Mimmaw, Aunt Ann,
and Grammaw Guthrie)

I dare not speak your name,
yet my heart whispers …
Momma
Since you left, the winters have grown colder
and springtime has lost it's splendor.
Somehow, Momma,
You've taken all the flowers.

I dare not speak your name,
yet my heart whispers …
Momma
I miss the sweet scent of you,
lilacs and honeysuckle springtimes
and cinnamon-scented winters.
At night my heart whispers,
in my dreams I call
and linger close at last,
holding dear
the last petal,
Your Smile …
the Rose of My Heart.

I shall not speak of you,
nor call your name out loud
until I get to glory,
the place where you abide.
No whisper from my heart you'll hear,
at last, a shout from deep inside …
Momma!

Love Abundantly

Life is loss. Life can be so difficult. And mixed up with all the hardships and difficulties are the people we love, the joy they bring us, and the hope we have in eternity.

Even Jesus wept at the death of his dear friend Lazarus.

Daddy's Arms

September 11, 2007

In daddy's arms there is a safety,
a humble, solemn peace.
There is laughter, warmth, and love inside
That's waiting just for me.

In daddy's arms I long to always be,
as storm clouds roll outside
And into daddy's arms I run
When from this world my heart must hide.

Why my dad was taken
At such a tender age
When love was oh so young and frail,
And Death turned daddy's way.

Yet we were never left alone,
God loves his children so.
My daddy is a child of God,
and in God's arms he rests,
Waiting, watching,
Praying till
The time God calls me home.

For into daddy's arms I'll run,
The circle now complete,
And in God's glorious light we'll stand,
My daddy, God, and me.

In daddy's arms there is a safety,
a humble, solemn peace.
There is laughter, warmth, and love inside,
Love eternally.

Love Abundantly

God cherishes those we love, especially in our absence.

"A father to the fatherless, a defender of widows, is God in his holy dwelling" (Ps. 68:5).

"But you, God, see the trouble of the afflicted; you consider their grief and take it in hand. The victims commit themselves to you" (Ps. 10:14).

This poem is dedicated to my big brother Wesley, who was killed July 3, 1983, by a drunken driver. Your children have turned out wonderful. I miss you.

Your little sis, Karen

A Good Thing, A God Thing

1999

I was born to a very fallible pair of parents. I was exposed to abusers and molesters. I never went to Disney World with my family. I went to bars and burglarized homes. I was in and out of foster homes and orphanages until I was in fourth grade.

The best of my early placements was with my grandmother and step-grandfather. He too assaulted me. I mention these facts of my early life, not as condemnations of my parents or God but as a point of reference for where God has brought me today.

All things work to the good for those who love God. I hope this is the message that is my past.

No matter what I have done or what has been done to me, I choose love …. God's love.

Life is about challenges and choices. We do not always have a choice about the challenges we face in life, but we do have a choice in how we face them.

I am sure that, to a lot of you, my life reads like a soap opera. In addition to enduring the abuses of my childhood, I am caring for my younger brother, who is paranoid, schizophrenic, and is dying of sclerosis of the liver and AIDS. My father died at age forty-seven from an alcohol-related heart attack.

My plans versus God's plans: my older brother, my hero, was killed by a drunk driver. He was killed by a man who was driving on a revoked license. After serving his six months for vehicular manslaughter, he was reportedly in the bars the day of his release, bragging about clearing the roads of motorcycle trash.

I can honestly say I hated that man. For ten years, on my brother's birthday, I would fantasize about calling him and wishing him a great day and telling him about my brother's two boys who were growing up without a father.

During those years, I graduated from college and began teaching. I taught art and had 750 students. I was having a ball. I got to play with kids and crayons all day long. What a great job! I had a thing called the Art Club. To become a member of the Art Club you didn't necessarily have to be talented; it was meant to give kids a boost, to help them feel better about themselves.

There was this very quiet fifth-grade girl. I'd had her in my class for three years. I had written her grades for countless art projects right next to her name, and it had never registered in my mind until one particular moment. I was writing her name on the certificate notifying her of her selection into the Art Club. And there it was. The same last name of the man who had killed my big brother. I looked up her file in the office, and he was indeed her father.

I went home with the worst headache of my life. All the pain, all the heartache, the memory of the scream, the sound that came out of me when I heard of my brother's death—everything came flooding back. I talked with my husband that night.

Could I, should I let her into the Art Club? If she found out our connection, how would that make her feel? Would she be hurt by the knowledge? Would I be able to look her father in the eyes or perhaps shake his hand if he should ever come up to school and thank me for having her in Art Club?

She would never even know that she had been considered for the club. It would never hurt *her* if I didn't let her in, but *I* would know.

I did not blame her for what her father had done. God knows how many times my own father had driven drunk. But what should I do? My husband told me he didn't know why I was even talking to him about it. He knew what I was going to do.

He was right. The next day, I called her out of class. She could not know what a sleepless night I'd had. I smiled at her. She squealed and jumped up and down, hugged me, and came to Art Club that afternoon.

I have pictures of her and me working on projects together. I kept focused on the purpose of the Art Club I had started. She needed to know she was special. It made me feel good.

God had helped me to do a good thing for her. No, that's wrong. God had done a good thing for me.

It was because of the time she and I spent together that God removed from my heart all of the anger and hatred I was carrying for her father. God healed the wound that I had picked at and nurtured for over a decade.

God had not brought me into her life to give her a boost. He had brought her into my life to teach me how to let go of the garbage and hold onto something good.

Now, instead of holding onto bitterness, hatred, and loss. I hold in my heart the memory of a young girl's smile and a hug.

Love Abundantly

"Whatever is true, noble, right, pure, lovely, admirable, excellent, or praiseworthy, think about such things" (Phil. 4:8).

I love my big brother. We went through so much together. I miss him dearly. But letting go of the hatred I felt for the man who killed him was very easy. All I had to do was focus on love, and God melted the hatred away.

Are you carrying pain or anger that prevents you from knowing God's true love for you? Prayerfully and lovingly find a way to let go of the ugliness and embrace God's love. This can be accomplished by prayer or, better yet, by showing God's love to an innocent yet deserving person. I promise you that God will bless you with peace and love.

For No Other Reason

December 18, 2007

For my husband, my friend, my Michael: There is no greater love than
that presented so tenderly each day by you. I love you today and always.
—Karen

Every beat of my heart
Every breath that I take
Every morning I rise
I look in your eyes
and go on,
for no other reason than love.

You lift me up,
help my heart to rise higher and soar …
for no other reason than love.

As pain gives way to sorrow,
you find my laughter, my joy
once again,
Ever holding me close, ever lifting me up,
my husband, my friend,
for no other reason than love.

Every beat of my heart
Every breath that I take
Every morning I rise
I look in your eyes
and go on,
for no other reason than love.

"My beloved is mine and I am his" (Song 2:16).
"This is my beloved, this is my friend" (Song 5:16).

A Hero's Song

July 11, 2008

When writing songs of good, great men,
Of heroes and their day,
We write of battles with dragons bold
And mythical, magical things
And sailors who claim their bounty
On oceans with sails as their wings.

In the footstep of a hero, is the measure of a godly man,
Yet a footprint is only a symbol
of what we leave behind.
Steadfast and true is my hero,
My hero, the light of my life,
Whose footprints you see are his legacy
Of true love and devotion.
As battle he does fearsome dragons,
He battles by day and by night.

Mystical dragons and magical swords
Are weapons of mythical knights.
My hero's sword is compassion, and humor is his knife.
He would not tell of dragons slain,
Nor boast of a hero's life,
He quietly tells of God's richest blessings,
Truest blessings, through all kinds of strife,
His blessings, his Savior, his children, his wife.

Some write of battles fought,
Of heroes bold, of wisdom wrought.
I write this song of a godly man
Who sails through life as the ocean.
My hero, my husband, my friend,
Whose compass is God,
Whose flame is love.
The wind in his sails is devotion.

Excerpts from letters to friends:

Dear Susana,
When we have something of value, we rarely appreciate its true worth. Such is the case with friendship. Our friendship has spanned over forty years. As with an item of value, the older this friendship is, the more priceless it becomes. Susana, your friendship is more valuable than any jewel I could ever possess. You are and ever shall be my friend. Your smile, laughter, and faith in God have been a treasured harbor to me. I just wanted to take a moment to tell you how much you are loved and valued.
Love, your pal, Karen

Dear Nancy,
There is a song in the heart of us all,
 whose melody is truth,
whose rhythm is written by God,
and whose lyrics are composed by those who love us.
And it is sung by our hearts to those we love.

We began our symphony first as student and teacher, moving to mentorship, and quickly to friendship. Your counsel during difficult times has been precious to me. You helped me see the value of my song in this world, and I love you.
Karen

To my friends,
God blesses us with relationships, both long- and short-term. He blessed Adam with Eve in the garden. He blesses us daily with those who would share our burdens. I have been so richly blessed throughout my life, but never as much as in these most difficult of times. You, my Christian family, have kept vigil, both in body and in prayer. You encourage me with comments on how I bless others. The truth is, I could do nothing without my Christ and my Christian family who have made him manifest in my life.

I thank you all. In Christ alone I rest. In him, all blessings are found.
Love, Karen Felton

Love Abundantly

"You and these people who come to you will only wear yourselves out. The work is too heavy for you; you cannot handle it alone" (Ex. 18:18).

"I will come down and speak with you there, and I will take of the Spirit that is upon them. They will help you carry the burden of the people so that you will not have to carry it alone" (Num. 11:17).

The true nature of a blessing is that you never know how much you bless others. Who has blessed you? Have you told them or others about your blessings? Share the stories; share the wealth.

A Mother's Prayer

September 23, 2007

Moment by moment our lives slip away,
Moment by moment God beckons come pray,
Share your dreams and desires,
Let your fears fall away,
for moment by moment I'm beside you,
every step, every heartbeat, every moment,
each day.

In one tender breathless moment,
you placed her in my arms.
I hold her close and breathe her in,
this new life,
innocence sublime,
mine on earth to treasure,
fashioned by the hand of God,
entrusted now to me, I wonder
at this gift from you,
this child, this wondrous ball of life.

May she find your heart and keep it close,
Guard her walk most tenderly.
May she find You there in answered prayer,
And love You so much more than me.
May she know in darkest moments
of your gentle, loving care.
No matter what her path in life,
may it circle back to Thee.

Moment by moment our lives slip away,
Moment by moment God beckons come pray,
Share your dreams and desires,
Let your fears fall away,
for moment by moment I'm beside you,
every step, every heartbeat, every moment, each day.

"The Lord your God is with you. He is mighty to save. He will take great delight in you. He will quiet you with his love. He will rejoice over you with singing" (Zeph. 3:17).

"You are my child, always. I delight in you." As you gaze into the eyes of your children, imagine yourself small and helpless. If you could hear one statement from God, what would you like to hear? Why?

Annie's Song, A Song of Grace

October 23, 2008

As gentle as a sparrow, you came into my life,
finding God in secret places,
simple pleasures, fallen leaves.
In the smile and tears and prayers of you, my friend,
In your eyes I've seen God's mercy,
His compassion and His grace.
In your smile His love abiding and His peace.
Faith, simple as the sunrise, perfect as the dew,
daily blessing and renewing, ever serving, ever giving,
ever in you, Christ is living.
God has blessed me with your friendship, ever true.

May God's holiness surround you,
keep you sheltered by His side.
May you find rest and comfort in His arms.
May God whisper to you always,
bring you peace and harmony.
Dear friend, whatever sorrows
you have hidden in your heart,
May God's grace and love surround you, set you free.

May you know that God has blessed me
Through those gifts you've given me.
As gentle as the sparrow, you came into my life,
finding God in secret places,
simple pleasures, fallen leaves.
In the smile and tears and prayers of you, my friend.

Love Abundantly

This song is dedicated to all my sisters in Christ who have comforted my weary body, dried my tears, and lifted my spirits through the past seventeen years. Annie, Terri, Karen, Patti, Diane, and Joy challenge me to be stronger in my faith, to have more prayer and praise time and to stay in the word.

"Your love has given me great joy and encouragement, because you, brother, have refreshed the hearts of the saints" (Philem. 7).

We all get weary sometimes. Has there been a time when you needed encouragement? Did someone encourage you? If yes, describe it. If no, how could you reach out?

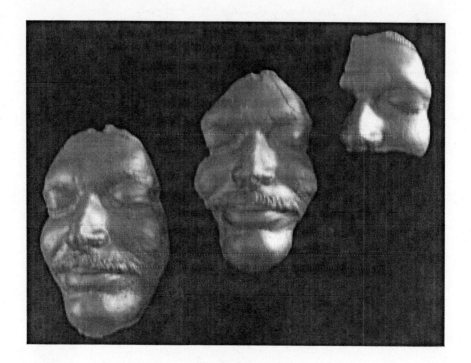

REVELATIONS

Revelations! – ceramic sculpture on wood, circa 1988
"Moses said to God, 'Suppose I go to the Israelites and say to them, "The God of your fathers has sent me to you," and they ask me, "What is his name?" Then what shall I tell them?'

"God said to Moses, 'I AM WHO I AM. This is what you are to say to the Israelites: "I AM has sent me to you."'

"God also said to Moses, 'Say to the Israelites, "The Lord, the God of your fathers—the God of Abraham, the God of Isaac and the God of Jacob—has sent me to you." This is my name forever, the name you shall call me from generation to generation'" (Ex. 3:13–15).

To love God, we must know him. To truly know God, we must spend time with him—time in the word, in prayer, in contemplation and praise.

This sculpture depicts the way my husband reveals himself to me more and more with each passing day. Such is the nature of God. As we face varying circumstances in our lives, he reveals his characteristics to us.

Choose at least three names on the "Getting to Know You" page. Tell how God revealed that aspect of himself to you.

1.

2.

3.

4.

5.

Getting to Know You

There is a lot in a name. When my husband's family first immigrated to America, their last name was spelled Felten. But during World War I, the spelling was changed to Felton, thus eliminating their ties to their German heritage. When selecting the name for a child, a grandmother gave sage advice. She suggested that the expectant mother stand on the front porch and yell the prospective name as loud as possible five times. If the mother is still happy with the name, then it is a good choice. I am convinced that middle names are given and used entirely for the purpose of striking terror in the hearts of children everywhere. Whenever I heard Karen Lynn Petty, I knew to run the other way because I was in trouble.

The first step in getting to know someone is the introduction. We meet, exchange names, and try to remember that name in hopes that when we meet again we will be able to recall it without too much embarrassment. Typically, when stuck on a name, we scroll through our memory: Is she from work? From my child's school? Church? Does she work at the dry cleaners? Is she the cop who gave me my last traffic ticket?

As we gain knowledge of God our Father, our judge, our provider, our Savior, we find comfort, courage, hope, and joy. Ephesians 1:4 tells us, "He chose us in him before the foundation of the world, that we should be holy and without blame before him in love." Jeremiah 1:5 states, "Before I formed you in the womb, I knew you."

Our father has intimate knowledge of who we are, and who we are to become in him. How can we possibly know God? He has revealed and continues to reveal himself to us daily through his word, prayer, obedience, faith, and his grace.

There have been times when my burden was so very heavy that I could not pray. It is during these times that I have relied totally on my father (Abba) to know the prayers of my heart. There have been times when my joy was so great that I could only cry out El Shaddai, my El Shaddai. I love you!

In the front of every Bible I own or give as a gift are written a few of the many names for God. They are there for those times when we have come to the end of ourselves and we reach for God, simply by calling his name. He knows the prayers of our hearts. Today as we worship God, let us call him by name, praising him for what he is, who he is.

El Shaddai	Almighty God (Gen. 17:1–20)
Jehovah Jireh	The Lord will provide (Gen. 22:13–14)
Jehovah Raah	The Lord is my shepherd (Ps. 23:1)
Jehovah (yhwy)	God, the infinite one
Eloi	My God
Abba	Father
I Am that I Am	God
Elohim	Strong One
Adonai	Lord
El Elyon	Most high strongest one (Isa. 14:13–14)
Yeshua	Jesus, Savior, Lord
Hosanna	Save we pray
Emmanuel	God is with us

Infinite – without end (1 Kings 8:27; Acts 17–24)
Eternal – free from the boundaries of time (Gen. 21–33)
Immutable – God is unchanging and unchangeable (James 1:17)
Omnipresent – God is everywhere (Ps. 139:7–12)
Omniscience – God knows all actual and possible things (Matt. 11:21)
Just – God is moral and fair (Acts 17:31)
Love – God loves us (Eph. 2:4–5)
Holy – God is holy and righteous (1 John 1:5)

Trust God

You cannot trust someone until you get to know them. You cannot know God unless you spend time with him.

Little Sister, Mine

February 14, 2007

Cascading memories of what love means to me.
Skipping rope and playing house,
Wedding bells and puppy dogs,
Flying kites and walking home from school.
And through it all I see
your eyes looking up at me,
Little one,
Little sister, mine.

Whispering winds and butterfly wings,
Cotton candy clouds and childhood dreams.
Flowers picked and bouquets brought
to self in cherished childish thoughts.
We will stand up in secret dance,
our songs in heart will thrive.
Courage paint our canvas bold,
In innocence, we will survive.
And through it all I see,
your eyes looking up at me,
Little one,
Little sister, mine.

As time begins its rage,
And youth gives way to age,
You take my hand and help me find my way.
I linger still on memory's bright hill,
Standing tall against the winds of time.
My memories rise of clearest blue skies,
A kite, two sisters, and a string.
Take hold my hand, my little one,
and upwards look, the clouds float by
On bluest ocean, you and I.
And through it all, I see your eyes looking up at me,
Little one, little sister, mine.

Love Abundantly

This poem was written for and given to my little sister Patti for Valentine's Day. We were separated for over twenty years. I am so glad we found each other, and I thank God for her every day. She helps and encourages me in ways she will never know. She has a tender servant's heart. I love her beyond measure.

Who do you love beyond measure? Is God at the top of your list?

"Love is patient, love is kind. It does not envy, it does not boast, it is not proud. It does not dishonor others, it is not self-seeking, it is not easily angered, it keeps no record of wrongs. Love does not delight in evil but rejoices with the truth. It always protects, always trusts, always hopes, always perseveres" (1 Cor. 13:4–7).

God is Love

"Take delight in the Lord, and he will give you the desires of your heart" (Ps. 37:4).

I guess I could be angry with God for taking so much away from me. I am not. He has made every moment so very precious to me.

Standing Joyfully

Twirling,

Spinning,

Flying,

Falling.

Holding trust in your hands

And hope in your heart,

And knowing
God is Love.

Love Abundantly

Several years ago I lamented to a friend that my son Michael has never known what it would be like to have a healthy Mom. I taught my daughter how to swim and how to play baseball, shagging out a line drive down the third-base line. But Michael always had to be "careful" around Momma.

I wept as I remembered twirling my daughter around till we were dizzy and tumbled to the ground. Last year I found these pictures taken by my husband. I had not remembered ever being able to do this with my son. Yet God had guarded the desires of my heart and gave them tenderly back to me.

With the photos came this whisper: "Your daughter had the blessing of your youth and strength. Your son is receiving the blessings of compassion and surrender.

To each of our children, we give separate blessings. What is the special blessing God has given you?

God is love.

Chapter Five
Ever Will I Praise Him Introduction

I have had my fair share of hardships and heartbreak. There were times when I did not feel God's presence in my life. Those seemed to be the easy times. I would not change the sweet, intimate hours spent with my Jesus for anything, although to be healthy for my husband would sorely tempt me.

Hope, I hope … that is still an alien word coming from me. Hope, I hope … they develop a cure for Parkinson's disease. I hope I can see the Grand Canyon with my husband. I hope I can travel to Africa, or better yet, hold and play with a grandbaby. I hope I can learn to tango. I really don't have a lot of earthly hope, but oh, how rich are my heavenly hopes.

Ever Will I Praise Him

May 1, 2010

Ever will I praise my Lord and King;
ever will I stand, ever will I sing,
ever will my soul in Him rejoice.

Who has formed the mountains
with his righteous hand;
who has paid the ransom for the sins of man?

Who has held me close when storm clouds roll;
who has ever soothed
the yearnings of my soul?

Whatever God has called, His will be done;
yearnings of my heart, my soul,
His kingdom come.

When on earth I breathe my last,
Awaken, O my soul, to sing in glory.
Ever will my heart delight in thee,
Ever will I sing the gospel story.

Old Chief and Warriors — Inked surface scratchboard, circa 1972

"Be happy, young man, while you are young, and let your heart give you joy in the days of your youth. Follow the ways of your heart and whatever your eyes see, but know that for all these things God will bring you to judgment" (Eccl. 11:9).

What the eyes have seen, the heart remembers. Things that we experience as a child often form who we are as adults. We spend so much time in the past. Do not allow yourself to be deformed by negative experiences. Rather, be transformed by the Holy Spirit. Know that God has been with you every step of every day. He loves you and wants to comfort and transform you.

What is a positive memory that helped form you?

What the eyes have seen
Remains hidden in the heart.
Ponies running on the open range.
Buffalo hunter
chieftain
warrior
old.
What the eyes have seen
Remains hidden in the heart.
A nation weeps
as its innocence is stolen
love
hate
victory
Surrender … all.
What the eyes have seen
Remains hidden in the heart.
Weep not for me,
but for
young warriors
all
lost
to destiny's
pride.
God sees …

Pencil drawing (replica), circa 1972, age seventeen
This drawing won a National Merit scholarship for me. We were poor, and
all I had to draw on was textured packing paper.

Watercolor on Bristol board, circa 1979

Bus Stop Memories

In the twilight of my life
I travel back
I remember
races won
love fulfilled
laughter of children
and always
God's loving hand around my shoulders,
now stooped in silent
solemn solitude.
Should I have died young?

How many would have mourned my passing?
Now that I am old,
is there no one to pray for me?
With me?

"Do not rebuke an older man but encourage him as you would a father,
younger men as brothers, older women as mothers, younger women as
sisters, in all purity"
(1 Tim. 5:1–2).

Live Boldly

Find someone to pray for, invest yourself in—the elderly, disabled,
someone who needs you.

Standing Before Him

1996

We stand before Him as a sparrow,
Adorned only with the colors of the earth
From which we were formed.
Humbly knowing
His love is eternal,
His grace is boundless.
Through His love we're formed,
By His grace we are transformed.

"Those who hope in the Lord will renew their strength. They will soar
on wings like eagles; they will run and not grow weary, they will walk
and not grow faint"
(Isa. 40:31).

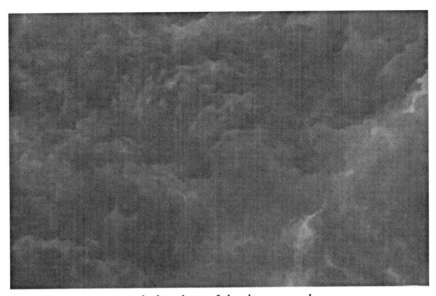

We took this photo of clouds over our home.
Can you see the image of crucified Christ and a lambs head under his arm.
September 12, 1987

In rolling clouds we hear the thunder,
See the lightning,
Taste the rain.

To a child all is known,
All is seen and heard and lived.
Each day is a moment,
Each breath is a lifetime.

In rolling clouds we hear the thunder,
See the lightning,
Taste the rain.

2005

There will be storms in our lives, and we will cry out, "Lord help me!"

We will sin, and we will call out, "Lord forgive me!"

We will, on occasion, rise above all and overcome.
We will stand as heroes in the eyes of the world.
It is in these times that we need God the most—
to ground us, to humble us, to love us.

1990

When I consider *hope*, I look at those who have gone before me and lived their lives with uncompromising hope and peace, and I know that God is in control.

My hope rests in Him alone.

When I consider *life*, I look at children playing, with no eye for color or economic class. I see life eternal.

When I consider *love*, I look at the cross and know that love has bridged the divide between God and man.

"As for me, I will always have hope; I will praise you more and more" (Ps. 71:14).

A Psalm of Praise

Published in church bulletin
Cornerstone Evangelical Free Church
March 17, 1996

Lord, in humility I stand before thee,
Offering only my deepest love for you.
In all of time,
Before my time,
And beyond my days,
You have loved me.
Lord, you know my strengths
(my times when standing in Your light).
You know when I fall (as the sparrow)
and lie in shame in the shadows before you,
and still You love me.

Father,
I tremble
In fear of your righteousness
with joy for your mercies.
Because of you,
I am carried on eagle's wings,
And I soar.

Abba, holy Father!
My heart is full,
You have loved me beyond
any earthly love.
I lift my life,
My heart, my soul,
My love to You.

"Are not two sparrows sold for a penny? Yet not one of them will fall to
the ground outside your Father's care. And even the very hairs of your
head are all numbered" (Matt. 10:29–30).

Livin' the Life of Lazarus

March 28, 2006

Livin' the life of Lazarus, livin' each day victorious,
 Seeing the sky with newly risen eyes.

I'm walking through tombs of darkness now,
 Yet never alone, to Him I bow.
I'm racing forth to praise His holy name,
 Knowing the tomb awaits me still,
 My body its only prize,
 Keeping this song my life's refrain,
 and gaze in His holy eyes.

Livin' the life of Lazarus, livin' each day victorious,
 Tasting the rain, and dancing in His word.

No promises has He made me now,
 The challenge before, stand true somehow,
 And witness to all of pain and victory,
 Broken for all the world to see,
Yet livin' to praise, His love has set me free.

Livin' the life of Lazarus, livin' each day victorious,
 hearing the songs of angels in the night.

Trust in His loving holiness,
 Seek joy in His holy tenderness,
 Live boldly in all we say and do.
 His lesson upon that holy tree,
 to carry the burdens joyfully
 Of others, and love abundantly,
 So that the world may see

We're
Livin' the life of Lazarus, livin' each day victorious,
Touching the wind with dreams we can't contain.
Livin' the life of Lazarus, livin' each day victorious,
Seeing the sky with newly risen eyes.
Livin' the life of Lazarus, livin' each day victorious,
Tasting the rain, and dancing in His word.
Livin' the life of Lazarus, livin' each day victorious,
Hearing the songs of angels in the night.

"When he heard this, Jesus said, "This sickness will not end in death.
No, it is for God's glory so that God's Son may be glorified through it"
(John 11:1–44).

Wings of Hope

June 9, 2006

Whispering winds of hope
rise up and lift my heart.
In hope I will dance with Him,
My God, lover of my soul.
Again my heart will sing
of his abiding peace
with hope lifted high,
In joy His praises I will sing.

Behold Him on the cross;
My sins he bore alone.
He stood before God's holy throne
That sin might ever die.
Borne on the wings of love,
Sweet melody of life
Eternally sings my heart of love
And victory through Christ.

When sorrow overtakes
My tender breathless heart,
I view the cross and love's sweet cost,
In victory I rise.
Now as hope shines through,
He bids me come and dance.
As morning dawns, hope is alive!
Darkest tears are gone,
With joyful praises will I rise.

What is your heart burdened with today?
Pray: "Lord, help me to rely on you and trust you more.
I know that everything I have is yours—
my wealth, my family, my health, all that I am. Especially lift my fears
concerning ..."

Trust God

"And he said unto his disciples, 'Therefore I say unto you, be not anxious for your life, what ye shall eat; nor yet for your body, what ye shall put on. For the life is more than the food, and the body than the raiment. Consider the ravens, that they sow not, neither reap; which have no store-chamber nor barn; and God feedeth them: of how much more value are ye than the birds!'" (Luke 12:22–24).

Before You. . .

8-29-06

Before You I come, Before You I bow,
Before You I am cleansed and forgiven,
As I kneel and pray before you every day,
I am called to consider life before you.

Before You in my sin I was lost eternally,
Blind to a peace that lay before me.
Before You, where was Hope?
.Where was Mercy? Where was Grace? Before You.

Before You I come, Before You I bow,
Before You I am cleansed and forgiven,
As I kneel and pray before you every day,
I am called to consider Worth, before You

.

Before You I was nothing, empty and alone,
Yet on that Holy Tree, poured out eternally
Now, forgiven and redeemed
I kneel Before You

As I kneel and pray before you every day,
May your power and your grace go before me.
May all who would see your grace and love in me
Feel my joy and surrender all before you.

Heaven's Lullaby

June 10, 2006

He bids me come,
He bids me rest,
Rest in His loving arms.
For in His arms are the wings of hope,
and echoed in His whisper every prayer.
In His love, we are lifted higher, carried on love's wings.
He bids me soar and linger evermore
in the precious heartbeat of my prayers.

He bids me come,
He bids me weep,
all my burdens share.
In prayer He comes nigh, singing heaven's lullaby,
and there in His heartbeat I find peace.
He bids me come and linger awhile
In a moment of prayer;
in that moment in time, I rest, sheltered from my fears,
resting in His lullaby of love.

He bids me come
and worship Him,
run to His loving arms.
He waits for me there by still water's shore,
His grace has been waiting evermore.
He bids me seek, find him, waiting there
for my moment of prayer.
Writing lullabies for me, love eternal sets me free,
in the precious heartbeat of my prayers.
"Come to me, all you who are weary and burdened, and I will give you
rest. Take my yoke upon you and learn from me, for I am gentle and
humble in heart, and you will find rest for your souls. For my yoke is
easy and my burden is light" (Matt. 11:28–30).

From the Ashes

July 16, 2006

Curse God and die;
how could they understand?
Borne on the sorrows of a holy, righteous man,
How deep His pain,
How infinite His love
That He might lose everything
and praise His God above.

Up from the ashes Job was lifted higher,
and from his sorrows he has been set free;
and as he whispered sweetly, Lord, I love you,
echoes of faith,
throughout eternity.

How would we fare?
Would we consider blessed?
How would we stand were we to face Christ's test?
And when He rose in sweet simplicity,
borne on the cross,
sorrows of a sinful world,
eternally.

Up from the ashes we are lifted higher
And from our sorrows, Christ has set us free;
And as he whispers sweetly, child, I love you,
echoes of love,
throughout eternity.

Live Boldly

How can we truly trust someone we do not know? God loves you and
wants nothing more than to spend time with you.
Today, each hour, prayerfully consider an individual line from the
Twenty-third Psalm, and at the end of each hour, write a few words
about what God has revealed to you.

Child of the Risen Savior

July 2006

I am a child of the risen Savior, Jesus Christ, the Lamb of God!
No earthly hand can claim me—I've been bought by Christ's dear blood.
On this lonely rock called Calvary, my Jesus stood alone,
and
claimed me for His own.

And I pray, Abba, my righteous Abba,
let Thy will be done;
and I pray, Abba, my righteous Abba,
until you call me home.

I am a child of the risen Savior, Jesus Christ, the Lamb of God!
No earthly hand can claim me—I've been bought by Christ's dear blood.
On this lonely rock called Calvary, my Jesus stood alone,
and claimed me for His own.

And I cry, Spirit, Holy Spirit
Use my flesh and bone;
and I cry Spirit, Holy Spirit,
until you call me home.

I am a child of the risen Savior, Jesus Christ, the Lamb of God!
No earthly hand can claim me—I've been bought by Christ's dear blood.
On this lonely rock called Calvary, my Jesus stood alone,
And claimed me for His own.

And I sing Jesus, my precious Jesus,
let my faith be strong.
And I sing Jesus, my precious Jesus,
until you call me home.
Father, Holy Spirit, precious Jesus,
Until you call me home.

Trust God

"For you know that it was not with perishable things such as silver or gold that you were redeemed from the empty way of life handed down to you from your ancestors, but with the precious blood of Christ, a lamb without blemish or defect" (1 Peter 1:18–19).
"Back Off, Satan!"

The hardest prayer for me to pray for my children was: "Father, let your will be done in their lives." We as parents want to keep our children safe, secure, and under our wings. God has a purpose for all of us. I wrote this song to remind myself that I am always God's child, and to tell Satan to *back off!* He has no power over me, my will, my body, or my faith.

In what area of your life do you need to tell Satan to *back off?* Through the power of God the Father, Christ the Son, and the holy and righteous Spirit, you can stand against the enemy.

Forever … Jesus

April 20, 2007

You are my strength;
You are my song;
You are my will to carry on.
You are my hope
when hope is gone.
You are Jesus,
My Jesus.

You are my comfort in a storm,
The light that keeps me ever warm.
In you I have no fear.
Forever, Jesus, you are near,
never ceasing, never ending.
You are my Savior forever, Jesus,
My Jesus.

You are my one redeeming call.
In you I stand and will not fall.
Forever sanctified I rise
to gaze forever in your eyes.
You are my Savior, one true friend.
You are Jesus, forever Jesus,
My Jesus.
And when my time on earth is through
and angels call me home to you,
forever I have always been loved most tenderly by thee.

My Jesus,
Precious Savior, Lord,
You are Jesus, forever Jesus,
My Jesus.

Still Waters

2010

Still waters, cool waters
Wash gently over me,
Bid me come be refreshed.
In His gentle eyes I see
reflections of
eternal love.
Oh, what bounties wait for me
in the water,
Christ's living waters.
Oh, the best is yet to be.

Whatever trial, whatever test,
Let wicked Satan do his best.
In Christ I'll rise,
Cast out the lies.
As angels sing in heaven glorious
My Jesus reigns, ever victorious,
As eagles soar and dip their wings
In waters cool and still.
Oh, Christ, my king,
with hope renewed,
Revived again I sing.
The best is yet,
is yet to be.

Trust God…

I have found encouragement and comfort from many places and people;
the most encouraging are those who help me find my answers and
comfort in God's Word.

Recently I have enjoyed listening to thirty-year-old radio broadcasts of
evangelists Joyce and Don R. Good. One of Don's favorite sayings was,
"The best is yet to come." I agree.
Where do you seek and find comfort and encouragement?

Cry Jesus

I cry Jesus, Living Water
Precious Savior, I thirst.
Praying, help me Lord to please you
and seek your holy face.
I'm a vessel, now your vessel,
broken by your grace.

Promises sweet promises,
Christ gave His life for these,
Jesus gave me water and life, eternally.
In life our thirst is constant
Our hunger is complete
the crown that grows so heavy,
we'll place at Jesus feet.
And on that day in glory
we'll stand as Christ's dear bride,
feasting with the angels,
and dancing in His light.

Promises sweet promises,
Christ gave His life for these,
Jesus gave me water and life, eternally.
His majesty shall touch the heart
of sinners one and all
and laying down His blood stained crown
Christ bore the penalty
No more shall sin and death prevail
Christ walked the very path to hell
And stands as ransom now,
In glorious victory.

I cry Jesus, Living Water
Precious Savior, I thirst.
Praying, help me Lord to please you
and seek your holy face.
I'm a vessel, now your vessel,
broken by your grace.

"But whoever drinks the water I give them will never thirst. Indeed, the water I give them will become in them a spring of water welling up to eternal life" (John 4:14).

Heaven Is a Heartbeat Away

As storm clouds roll,
Hope eternal
Whispers.
Dear soul,
Come near,
Hear Him.
Heaven is a heartbeat away.

In tempest rage
Fears of the age rush in.
Take courage, my friend.
Hope eternal
Beckons your soul.
See Him.
Heaven is a heartbeat away.

Burdened souls, wounded by sin,
Born again,
Reach out. Touch Him.
and find,
Heaven is a heartbeat away.

Trust God

"Our father which art in heaven, Hallowed be thy name, Thy
kingdom come, Thy will be done in earth, as it is in heaven.
Give us this day our daily bread, And forgive us
our debts, as we forgive our debtors.
And lead us not into temptation, but deliver us from evil: For thine is the
kingdom, and the power, and the glory, for ever. Amen" (Matt. 6:9–13).

Today, contemplate how close God and eternity with Him truly are.

Tender Mercies

December 7, 2006

May God stand with you in the sunshine,
shelter you in the rain.
May He dance with you in your joyful hours,
and hold you close in your pain.

In all of time there is nothing new
that we could ever conceive.
Now flowing through is God's sweet love,
if only we will believe.

May God stand with you in the sunshine,
shelter you in the rain.
May He dance with you in your joyful hours,
and hold you close in your pain.

He who began a good work in you,
will never turn away.
In the darkest tempest, His love is there,
look closely and you will say ...

My God stood with me in the sunshine,
Sheltered me in the rain.
He danced with me in my joyful hours,
and held me close in my pain.

Yes, He stands with me in the sunshine,
shelters me in the rain.
He dances with me in my joyful hours,
and holds me close in my pain.

"Being confident of this, that he who began a good work in you will carry it on to completion until the day of Christ Jesus" (Phil. 1:6).

Live Boldly

One way to live boldly during difficult times is to climb out of yourself and pray for others.
I wrote this prayer and said it over each of the five hundred blankets I made in 2008. I prayed for each person who would receive a blanket from me.
I prayed the same prayer in 2009 and 2010 when praying for over 420 people who allowed me the honor of drawing their portrait.

Who can you pray for today?

Trust God

"For God, who said, 'Let light shine out of darkness,' made his light shine in our hearts to give us the light of the knowledge of God's glory displayed in the face of Christ" (2 Cor. 4:6).

The Lighthouse

Dedicated to Shirley Felton
January 21, 2008

There is a lighthouse that lights the path
of ships and sailors on darkest seas.
It is a beacon of hope and safety
and bids all to come home,
come rest.

There is a lighthouse on the hillside
brightly burning, safe from dangers
of rock and tide.
It is a beacon of blessed salvation
and bids all to come home, come rest.

There is a lighthouse in Christian hearts
that lights the way
for weary souls in tempest gale;
there is a peace and a blessed salvation.
As the Spirit Holy bids,
come home, come rest

Oh, Christ, my Lighthouse,
Lord, I am so weary,
yet in your light I'm renewed.
Oh, Christ, my Lighthouse,
my blessed salvation.
Lord, in Your Light
I am renewed,
And
with joy I will go on singing
Until the day when I hear you call,
" Come home, weary child. Come rest."

Always

February 3, 2008

Every morning I rise and praise Your name,
singing always a love song to You.
Every morning I long to be renewed.
Let me be a blessing,
rise and be a blessing to you.

In the stillness and the heartbeat of the night,
sometimes it's hard to do what we know is right.
You're always there to guide us and forgive,
we fall short, we all fall short,
we all fall short—of the glory of God.

How holy is Your love, how perfect is your grace.
For God so loved the world. It is true,
once for all my Jesus died for me.
And now I know in Jesus I'm set free.

Resting in His love for eternity,
His peace and assurance I've received.
My Jesus is alive.
Now I live and sing as one redeemed.

Every morning I rise and praise Your name,
Singing always a love song to You.
Every morning I long to be renewed.
Let me be a blessing,
Rise and be a blessing to you.

"A psalm of Asaph. The Mighty One, God, the Lord speaks and
summons the earth from the rising of the sun to where it sets" (Ps. 50:1).

Aunt Jean

How blessed to have known her,
   this woman of God,
   Vision of His presence,
   reflecting His love.

There lived an angel
who walked among men.
We called her our Mother,
Grammaw, Mimmaw, Aunt,
   Friend.

The thought of tomorrow
   without her loving face
   makes life ever lonely,
   a sad, solemn place.

Gone is our sunshine,
   our roses from God,
our dewdrops from heaven,
   our song from above.

Yet we must remember,
how brief life can be
this side of heaven
for you and for me.

One day God will call us
to be by His side,
To walk in His shadow,
to live as His bride.

Again we will see her,
in her arms we'll be blessed
as she beckons toward heaven,
come home child, come rest.

Precious in the sight of the Lord is the death
of his faithful servants" (Ps. 116:15).

Watching Over You

March 13, 2008

I'm no angel … simply momma.
God knows that it is true,
but with the angels sent from God,
I'm watching over you.

You'll feel me in the whispering winds
of a silent winter's night.
My arms around your soul, dear ones,
holding you so tight.

I did not leave you willingly.
My work on earth was through.
Now your time has come to dance,
For you're a momma, too.
So light your baby's way with love,
Tell them of you and me,
Tell them of their God above,
Who loves us all so tenderly.

Know I'm there in lonely hours
when you're sad and blue.
Know with all your heart,
I'm proud, so proud of you.

Of all the things I might have been
And all the things I've done,
to have been your momma and been loved by you
was my special gift from God.
My precious gift was *you*.

"How priceless is your unfailing love, O God! People take refuge in the shadow of your wings" (Ps. 36:7).

Shadows

July 7, 2008

Shadows, precious shadows,
hiding in the shadows of His wings.
For in the shadows there, my Jesus waits
for me,
praying someday from the shadows we're set free.
In the shadow of the eagle's wings
we are lifted and renewed.
In the shadow of a rock cleft by God that you may see,
He shields us from His glory
till that time when we're
set free.

Shadows, precious shadows,
hiding in the shadows of His wings.
For in the shadows there,
my Jesus waits for me,
praying someday from the shadows we're set free.
It was in the shadows, too,
my Christ was crucified.
As his blood fell to the earth,
shadows filled the bright, clear sky,
and a cry came from the shadows of that
cross on Calvary:
Father, why have you forsaken me?
Please forgive them. It is finished. Can't they see?

Shadows, precious shadows,
hiding in the shadows of His wings.
For in the shadows there, my Jesus waits for me,
praying someday from the shadows we're set free.

Eagles Rising

June 18, 2008

There is a stillness in the air,
as we draw near to God in prayer.
In His arms He bids
come home, come rest.

All your battles now are through,
come sit, just me and you;
by still waters' soothing shore,
we'll talk of days gone by
as I call thee now to Me.

I can see the eagle rising,
I am sheltered by its wings,
as I freely soar toward the distant blue.
My life I see before me.
My sins are now exposed,
redeemed and forgiven
I'm set free.

Seeing now the smile I've yearned for,
my Christ, in glory standing,
in my fondest dreams, I've seen Thee,
holy Savior, precious Jesus,
my sweet Lord.

Oh, to see His holy face,
to take His hand and hear the words,
Come home my faithful servant,
well done, come home, come rest.

There is a stillness in the air
as we draw near to God in prayer.
In His arms He bids come home,
Come rest.

Trust God

This poem was given to me by God before undergoing my second of three shoulder surgeries. I remember writing only a few lines, and after I returned home from the hospital I found it on my PDA.

God writes a lot about eagles. If you have ever been close to an eagle and felt the wind from its wings brush over you, you know the power and strength of the eagle. Most people don't notice how perfectly silent the eagle is.

The eagle flies:
stealthy, steady, strong,
bending its will to no man,
surrendering all to the wind.

The eagle glides:
ethereal, eternal, enduring,
pinions fashioned by God,
gleaning distance and velocity from turbulence.

The eagle sees:
fixed, focused, fierce.
There is no guile, no pity, only pride
reigning.

Swooping
diving
delighting
in singular creation
God is …

Read these scriptures: Exodus 19:4; Deuteronomy 32:1; Isaiah 40:31. Consider each scripture, as they describe different characteristics of God. Which is your favorite verse and characteristic?

Miracles

August 1, 2008

Elohim, the Creator ...
When the world began,
You spoke and formed the heavens, sea, and land.

Eloi, my God ...
In Your image we were fashioned
as You breathed Your very essence into man.

Jehovah-Rapha, Lord who heals ...
As disease steals all my hopes and dreams,
is there no turning destiny?

Abba, Father God ...
Oh, Father God in heaven, is there no miracle for me?
I know He healed the leper,
made the lame to walk,
helped the blind man see.
Oh, Father God in heaven, is there no miracle for me?

When in my heart I question the value of my life,
what value is there, God, in death?
Where is the dignity?
How can a kind and loving God ask so much of me?
In brokenness I come,
in that brokenness I see.

Jehovah-Shammah, the Lord is there ...
Standing in the garden, forsaken and alone,
kneeling now in prayer:
Father, take this cup, let it pass from me.

EL-Shaddai, the All-Sufficient …
In courage glory rises.
He stands to walk alone
and calls out to His Father,
thy will, not mine, be done.

Jehovah-Raah, the Lord, my Shepherd …
A crowd now mocks His holiness;
take Him, crucify
this prophet! He must die.

El Roi, God who sees …
Blood flowed from His wounded flesh,
thorns now pierced His brow,
all life's pain and sorrows reflected in his eyes.
Carrying His cross—my sins—He stumbles and He falls.
Yet in His courage, glory rises
from the blood-soaked soil that day,
and walk he did, the path for frail humanity.

Jehovah-Jireh, the Lord will provide …
Redefining dignity,
nailed upon that cross,
bloodied and in solemn solitude He cries,
Father, why have you forsaken me?

Adonai, Lord Master …
In courage glory rises,
My Savior breathes His last.
Father, please forgive them,
they know not what they do.
It is finished.

El Olam, Everlasting God …
El Elyon, God Most High …
As his temple that is my body crumbles before my eyes …

Yahweh, Lord …
I know he healed the leper,
made the lame to walk,
helped the blind man see.
Oh, Father God in heaven,
I praise you for this miracle,
My Christ who died for me.

"Who has known the mind of the Lord? Or who has been his counselor? Who has ever given to God, that God should repay them? For from him and through him and for him are all things. To him be the glory forever! Amen" (Rom. 11:34–36).

Blessed Be …

February 8, 2010

With all that is in me, I stand and seek His face.
With all that is in me now, I sing.
Blessed be, oh, blessed be,
Yahweh, Holy God,
Whose plan I dare not see.
Bless my heart that I might be
a blessing now to Thee.
Blessed be, oh, blessed be,
blessed be the name of the Lord.

Through sorrow still I sing.
Oh, Father, blessed be
yours to give and take away.
In this darkest hour I see
my Christ who gave His all, poured out to pardon me.
My Christ, Emmanuel,
in whom all sinners' hope does dwell.
Raise voices now to sing in victory.
Holy Spirit by my side,
Give me strength, be my guide,
teach me now that I might be
a blessing, Lord, to Thee.

With all that is in me, I stand and seek His face.
With all that is in me now, I sing.
Blessed be, oh, blessed be,
Yahweh, Holy God,
Whose plan I dare not see.
Bless my heart that I might be
a blessing now to Thee.
Blessed be, oh, blessed be,
blessed be the name of the Lord.

Sweet Spirit

July 6, 2008

There is a sweet, sweet spirit standing by;
He awaits our prayers most patiently.
Oh, hear the angels sing
When we come to Him in prayer.
Holy Abba,
Precious Jesus,
My sweet Spirit, Savior, Lord.

How tender are the moments
When in brokenness I come.
As I stand with all that's in me
and I sing,
He meets me there
to lift me evermore.
In one quiet earthly moment
I am cradled in His arms.
I can hear his righteous heartbeat
in my dreams
and my hour of need.
By still waters' soothing shores,
as the eagle soars above me,
I'm set free,
and still I rise again
through faith
and hope alone.
For in His shadow
I am sheltered, renewed.

There is a sweet, sweet spirit standing by;
He awaits our prayers most patiently.
Oh, hear the angels sing
When we come to Him in prayer.
Holy Abba,
Precious Jesus,
My sweet Spirit, Savior, Lord.

"In the same way, the Spirit helps us in our weakness. We do not know what we ought to pray for, but the Spirit himself intercedes for us through wordless groans. And he who searches our hearts knows the mind of the Spirit, because the Spirit intercedes for God's people in accordance with the will of God" (Rom. 8:26–27).

One Thread

November 9, 2008

Rise up, feel the glory,
reach out, touch His grace.
With all that is in me, I will seek His holy face,
To touch just one thread, before Him humbly bow.
Lord, I need your saving grace,
Sweet Father, lift me now.

As it was so long ago, so it is for me:
from my sin-soaked body, I beg you set me free.
Oh, but for my Savior's love
who guides and strengthens me.

Rise up, feel the glory,
reach out, touch His grace.
With all that is in me, I will seek His holy face,
To touch just one thread, before Him humbly bow.
Lord, I need your guiding hand,
Sweet Spirit, guide me now.

Raindrops and teardrops fall from above,
Precious deliverance, God's glory and love.
"Who touched me?" he called
as my tears fall like rain.
Who touched me?
My soul hungers still.
"Who touched me?" he calls out
In glorious refrain.
Who touched me? as nailed to the cross He was slain.

Rise up, feel the glory,
reach out, touch His grace.
With all that is in me I will seek His holy face,
To touch just one thread, before Him humbly bow.
Sweet promise, in your love I rest,
sweet promise, hold me now.

I wrote this poem during times when the crushed shoulder bone kept dying, and I was in indescribable pain. I dropped this poem and it slid under my chair when I fell asleep. I couldn't sleep in bed, the pain was so horrible.

I was home from the hospital and on so much pain medication I could barely walk. I fell and broke three ribs, but while on the floor, I saw and retrieved this forgotten poem.

Never think: "It can't get much worse." It can.

People would ask me how I was doing, and I said simply, "I'm still here, and the good news is … when I'm not, I'll be there (in heaven)."

"One thing I ask from the Lord, this only do I seek: that I may dwell in the house of the Lord all the days of my life, to gaze on the beauty of the Lord and to seek him in his temple" (Ps. 27:4).

The Promise

December 28, 2009

There's a promise waiting for me on the hillside.
'Tis a promise made so very long ago:
made before the earth began,
made before the times of man.
A promise whispered in the night
on angel's wings.

Oh, how tenderly this promise God fulfilled
on the Christmas morning oh-so-long ago,
Not in glorious victory, but in frail humanity.
This precious promise
placed so tenderly in her aching arms,
His mother Mary weeps,
as God, the promised, so tenderly now sleeps.

Now in His holiness I see
a promise broken now for me.
Torn from that rugged cross
on a hill called Calvary,
as they placed Him in her aching arms,
his mother Mary weeps,
as in death's darkest tomb
her promise now must sleep.

Borne on the sins of man,
God's holy righteous plan,
no sin nor worldly thought could make him bow.
'Twas the love He had for me
that nailed my promise to that tree.
This same promise stands, my Lord, Emmanuel.

There's a promise waiting for me, on the hillside.
'Tis a promise made so very long ago,
made before the earth began,
made before the times of man.
A promise whispered in the night on angel's wings.

Rainbows

October 31, 2009

Hope never ceasing,
she sees the world in His eyes.
He takes her hand as they walk ever slowly,
slowly through rainbows in time.

Days mark the decades,
and heartbeats the hours.
Hear now her heartbeat, her cry;
hear now the thunder, see now the lightning,
taste now the rain as she cries.

Weary and broken, in faith persevering,
see her humbly now rise.
Dancing in rainbows to God's holy rhythm,
knowing and living through Him,

beyond all her sorrow He stood ever strong, ever true,
true to the promise of rainbows from teardrops,
teardrops her Savior once shed.
Now these same precious teardrops
roll ever silent,
roll from her heart to His hand.

Days mark the decades
and heartbeats the hours.
Hear now her heartbeat, her cry;
He tenderly holds her teardrops and sorrows,
calming the storms in her heart.
Now in His comfort, she's dancing forever,
dancing through rainbows in time.

Hope never ceasing, she sees the world in His eyes.
He takes her hand as they walk ever slowly,
slowly through rainbows in time.

Seek Joy

We all have storms in our lives. Instead of blaming God for the storms, try thanking Him for bringing you through the storms and into the rainbow.

"Then I saw another mighty angel coming down from heaven, wrapped in a cloud, with a rainbow over his head, and his face was like the sun, and his legs like pillars of fire" (Rev. 10:1).

Have you ever tried to make a rainbow using a hose? I used to love doing this as a child. On a hot day, refracted light can make small "personal" rainbows.

On your next warm day, make rainbows with a friend. Share with each other how God has encouraged you during difficult times.

Now I Know I'm Not in Heaven

This poem was written after my seventh major surgery in two years. I woke up during surgery, but could not speak or communicate with my doctors. I listened as my doctors spoke about after-work plans and discussed patients who "bled out" and died under similar surgical circumstances. I felt blood running down the back of my neck; I heard the anesthesiologist tell the doctors they had "better do something. Her blood pressure is dropping really fast!" I thought, well, it's my birthday. I guess I get to see Jesus on my birthday.

Later I woke in recovery and saw the sweet faces of my husband and mother-in-law and disappointedly mumbled, "Now I know I'm not in heaven." I have since apologized to both Mike and his mom.

For an Instant

October 14, 2008

For an instant in His arms He held me.
For an instant in His care alone, my soul was free.
All my life I've longed to see
my Jesus smile at me
And to run into his arms as He whispers
"Oh, beloved, you are mine."

For an instant stand we now as one
before God's holy throne,
and on that gentle brow I see
a crown of thorns laid there by me
as His blood flows to the ground,
a tear falls silently.
He boldly then proclaims,
All her sins are mine alone;
all is silent save the beating of His heart.

For an instant in His arms he held me
for an instant in His care alone
my soul was free.
Yet in one silent solemn instant
He breathed life back into me.
Still more to be done,
till my Christ shall call me home;
not for an instant
but home eternally.

Joy in Suffering

November 1, 2009

To walk with angels, weep with God.
To soar on eagles' wings,
to die with Christ and daily bring
this cross to bear my suffering.

Weep not in sorrow for my losses, but in joy I sing
praise to my Christ, whose blood was shed
for all the sins that bound me.
For 'tis the cross that set me free,
and there my Jesus found me.

Weep not in sorrow for my losses
but in joy for the crosses.
The shadow of the cross reveals
God's mercy, grace, and peace,
His love enduring evermore
as suffering brings surrender,
surrender brings release.

Weep not in sorrow for my losses but in joy for the crosses.
For in agony I've seen
my Savior crucified,
and tasted I the salt
of my Savior's tears.

Bittersweet this offering my Jesus gave for me.
Death's wicked sting I'll face no more.
His love has set me free.

Weep not in sorrow for my losses,
But in joy I sing.
Praise to my Christ whose blood was shed
for all the sins that bound me.
For 'tis the cross that set me free,
and there my Jesus found me.

"For his anger lasts only a moment, but his favor lasts a lifetime; weeping may stay for the night, but rejoicing comes in the morning" (Ps. 30:5).

Song of Africa

November 9, 2009
For my friend Pam, who left her footprint and heart in Africa.

Africa, oh Africa,
Forever will my heart sing
your song, oh Africa.
Does my heart not quicken
with each rising sun,
and
faintly grows my longing heart
as the sun now sets.

Africa, oh Africa,
To drink in bold aromas of the Serengeti,
to feel the warmth of the sun
by day
and the cool whisper of God
at night.

Africa, oh Africa,
How I have dreamed of you!
In sleepless dreams I walk
to witness now this perfect land,
canvas painted boldly,
richly,
by the Master's hand.

Africa, oh Africa,
hear now,
written on your wind,
the call of the lioness.
Feel the earth tremble
beneath the feet of the elephant.
Witness again the graceful saunter
of the giraffe.

Africa,
that I might leave behind
a solemn footprint
and for an instant
be a part of you.

Africa, oh Africa,
Where else on earth
is God more immediate,
more glorious, more infinite?

Africa, oh Africa,
You do not know me,
Yet how I have loved thee,
Africa.

I Am

May 18, 2010

The Lord smelled the pleasing aroma
And made a covenant with man.
A rainbow he struck in the heavens,
A promise before time began.
Imagine heaven, aromas holy and pleasing to God.
Then as floodwaters receded, God with His infinite plan
said, Build an altar
To worship me,
Unchanging, eternal,
I Am

Look
See now the oceans I have formed,
Breathe in the cool evening breeze,
Hear now my heartbeat,
Tides pounding, my rhythm. Proclaiming my majesty
I Am

Listen
Hear now the voices
Great leaders, present, past
Appointed to rule over time and destiny.
I have lifted them high, I have cast them down.
All will bow, all will cry out,
Holy and just
I Am

Taste
The sweetness of my bounty
Here at the table I have prepared for you.
Come taste bitter herbs of your sins,
Now forgiven and forgotten.
The Lamb of God, Holy Christ, Savior, Spirit, God
Now drink in the sweet nectar of redemption
And know eternally,
You are mine.
Touch, reach out,
Not with your hands but with your heart.
Believe
Know that I love you
And know that
I Am

9/II

<u>A</u> date written on the clouds of time—
as a nation we watched and wept,
as families we held our breath and each other,
and our innocence was lost forever,
stolen by an evil too large for any of us to comprehend.
In the thunder of a boot print on dust and debris,
a fireman stands his ground,
By God,
and guts, and will.
<u>M</u>any sought to defeat us by murdering innocence,
discovering the incomprehensible,
that grace and courage grow on godly ground.
<u>E</u>vil stood and looked us in the eye,
we did not flinch,
the earth trembled as the towers fell,
and yet
it was evil that could not look the world in the eyes.
It was evil that hid behind a mask and the bodies of innocents.

Remember always the courage of 9/11,
when a nation was brought to its knees,
not by fear, but in prayer.
Inherent in the will of this nation,
a strength that is insurmountable,
Courage that is unquenchable.
America ... remember!
The mournful widows' cries,
the cadence of the death roll, and photos on the wall.
May we not forget our heroes born that fateful day,
Policemen, firemen, soldiers—heroes all
Who stood their ground.
In the thunder of a boot print, on sandy foreign soil,
a soldier stands his ground today
By God
and guts
and will.

"Have I not commanded you? Be strong and courageous. Do not be afraid; do not be discouraged, for the Lord your God will be with you wherever you go" (Josh. 1:9).

Dancing With God

When I was younger and healthier, I used to go outside when everyone else in the house was fast asleep. Sometimes before dawn, sometimes at midnight, sometimes at sunset. I don't know if any neighbors saw me, or what they thought I was doing.

I would begin slowly spinning, turning and bowing to God. My arms would be stretched outward, palms turned toward heaven. In my head and sometimes aloud, I would recite the 148th Psalm. Depending on the time of day and year, I would call on various things around me to praise God with me. I haven't been able to do my dance in oh-so-long; it is a very intimate time between God and me.

But when alone and in pain, I close my eyes and I still dance with God. Try it. God will bless you, I promise. Oh, don't worry about your neighbors. Go! Dance with God!

Psalm 148

"Praise the Lord. Praise the Lord from the heavens,
praise Him in the heights above,
"Praise Him, all His angels, praise Him, all His heavenly hosts.
"Praise Him, sun and moon, praise Him, all you shining stars.
"Praise Him, you highest heavens and you waters above the skies."

Delight

Praise Him, all you mountains,
praise Him rocks, earth, and sea.
Lift your voices with the angels.
God in heaven takes such delight in thee.

Turning, turning, turning
pages throughout time,
symphonies of morning light.
God, please guide me through this day;
help me Lord to always be precious in Your sight.

Praise Him, oh, you cold, cold wind,
praise Him fallen leaves,
birds upon the branches, eagles in the air
lift your wings and voices now with symphonies above,
lift them now to soar with love.
We lift them, Lord, to Thee.

Praise Him, turning seasons,
praise Him, sun and rain.
Oh, Father God in heaven,
hear now our symphony
as rocks cry out Your glory, Lord,
and angels' voices rise.
I, too, humbly lift my voice
and sing beneath your moonlit skies.

Holy, holy, holy
Lord, God Almighty,
infinite in power and love,
each day this love I see.
Holy, holy, holy,
Holy Spirit, guide me.
Shield me from this sinful world.
Help my offering be
sweet aroma, pure and bright,
precious in God's holy sight.
Holy, holy, holy,
precious risen Savior,
each day please hear my plea.
I cannot wait for heaven,
no crown of jewels to bring to you,
yet bending down, this simple crown
of love I give Thee.

Praise Him all you mountains,
praise Him rocks, earth, and sea.
Lift your voices with the angels.
God in heaven takes such delight in thee.

Simeon and the Cross

Testimony Given at church
and Women's Correctional Facility
July 14, 2006

We are called each day to pick up our cross and boldly carry it in the pursuit of holiness.

What cross do we carry each day? What burden is placed on our lives that we may carry to our Lord? Is it the darkness of depression? Abuses suffered at the hands of others? The burden of our own sins or concerns for our children, devastating illness or the loss of a loved one?

Whatever that loss, we are all called to willingly carry that cross entrusted to us by God.

I try very hard to live up to God's challenge, and I fail miserably every single day. I am a fraud. Everyone thinks I am so brave, heroic, and strong. I know how weak and fallen I am, and so does my loving Father and Savior. The world does not see the fraud in me.

Jesus on his journey to the cross stumbled. He was too frail to carry the physical burden of his cross. Simeon was charged to carry Christ's physical cross. I compare myself only with Christ's weakness. Yet it is in that weakness that God has provided my Simeons. My Simeons are my testimony. They help me see the heart of my Jesus in their eyes.

My Simeons are the children I have had in my Sunday school classes. Some are grown and tower over me and speak to me in quite deep voices: "Mrs. Felton, I am praying and fasting for you." They write me letters thanking me for teaching them. They encourage and strengthen me.

My Simeons are the little ones whose sweet simple prayers are: "Dear God, make Mrs. Felton well again."

My Simeon is my sister who drives an hour every day to help with my house and to help care for me and my family.

My Simeons are friends like Terri, Shannon, and Karen, who come to my home and pray with and for me, and who help me laugh at myself when pitiful has outlived its welcome.

My Simeons are the many people here at Cornerstone Church who have helped in so many immeasurable ways—from providing meals, to late night phone conversations when I was feeling so sick and alone.

My Simeons are the many people who every year help me do the thing that brings me great joy: teach Sunday school. We are a church of Simeons. I think somehow we may have forgotten this fact. I am proudest of our church for this.

I want to focus my testimony on God's grace by providing me with two specific Simeons.

I have taught here at Cornerstone for over ten years; I have left hospital beds to teach Sunday school. I am driven by a desire to teach young people about the God who first loved me. My passion is the Bible and that our children understand that his Bible is a tremendous love letter from God to them. Last year my struggle with Parkinson's got very, very scary. Mike and I even discussed assisted living for me. A great deal of my day was spent in agony. This was not new to me. What was new was my inability to feed and dress myself. My speech was becoming compromised and I could not even turn over in bed. I had stopped teaching art. I had stopped working.

On a solemn Sunday morning in May, I had planned to come in and tell my class and fellow teachers that I simply could not teach any longer. I was weary.

God had other plans. Earlier that morning, a student I had ten years earlier had gone into my classroom and filled the black board with every encouraging scripture imaginable. She was going through terrible heartaches of her own, yet God used her to encourage me. I jokingly asked my co-teachers, "If I do not make it in on some Sunday, can you take over for me?" "Sure," was their reply. "When I do show up," I asked them, "can you let the Holy Spirit take over and get out of our way?" "Sure," they said.

My Simeon, my husband—our walk is filled with wonderful contradiction, finding laughter though pain, victory through surrender. Every day he works at his job, providing for our family. He often travels. When he gets home, he works to keep our home sound and secure. He does laundry and dishes, cooks and cleans, and cares for me in my suffering. He loves me beyond measure.

My husband—my friend who daily, quietly, and gently carries my cross— is my Simeon and is deserving of much more than my love. Yet that is all I have to offer, and I know it is enough.

These days I feel very much as Lazarus must have felt. The results of the brain surgery have been remarkable. I am still in bed a great part of the day, but when I am up and moving, how wonderful it is. Mike and I are going for walks around the block and are able to sit side by side in church.

This is not a cure. I still have advanced Parkinson's disease, and it will continue its ugly march against my body. There will come a time when these devices will no longer block the symptoms of the disease. Every six months, the doctors will turn the devices off so that I can see how bad I am getting. I welcome these reality checks.

Like Lazarus, I know what tomb ultimately awaits my body. I like to think that Lazarus looked at the world through different eyes. My sense of urgency is greater to live, to do, and to teach.

I will continue to need my Simeons in my life, to help me do that which I love: to tell others about our Christ. I thank you all for being that part in my life, my testimony that I accept and embrace, that part which is God's.

May we all be blessed by needing a Simeon in our lives, by God providing each of us with a Simeon, and by the wisdom to recognize the blessings of frailty, strength through weakness, and the victory of surrender.

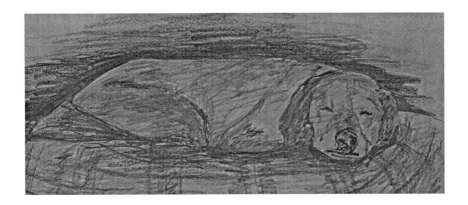

You Have Such a Face

May 15, 2008

In remembering, we often face a part of ourselves only God and we are aware of. As I contemplate the past few years, I am struck with the certain understanding that if we will only listen, God is always speaking to us.

One of those times was a Sunday morning about six years ago. It was January 2002. I was in tremendous pain and could not make it to my van to get to church. Mike offered to carry me to the van, but the pain was too great, as was my feeling of uselessness.

I was awaiting the placement of my service dog, Gidget. I could not get out of bed to get a glass of water. Gidget was being trained to bring things from the fridge, get the phone, and much more, but she was not yet placed with me.

This particular day, I was feeling useless and fearful. I cried out, "God, who will love me when I can no longer take care of myself? When I am useless and can no longer teach or help others?"

I had a good, long, lonely cry that morning. My old lab mix Molly jumped up in my bed. She rarely did this, so it really got my attention. Talk about useless. I thought, you cannot do anything for me. I assailed poor Molly with all her uselessness and faults. She simply looked lovingly into my eyes, into my very soul.

Her unconditional love broke my cycle of sadness and self-pity. I looked into her loyal, loving eyes and said to her, "Molly, I don't need you to do anything for me. You are useless to me. Oh, how I love you, Molly. You have such a face."

Suddenly those became God's words to me. Karen, I don't need you for anything. There is nothing you can do for me. All you have to do is love me and to be loved by me. Oh, sweet child, how I love you. You have such a face. If we listen, we will hear *whispers* from a loving God.

This poem is dedicated to every woman who has survived injustice, racism, abuse, or persecution, the woman who survives with her faith and character intact.

It is inspiration derived from heartache and the inability to understand the actions of a friend. It is a slam against the author of mankind's cruelty and sin. My first response was to cry; my heart truly was broken. I was defenseless against the lies. God led me back to his lap, asking, "What do you want the world to see in you? If you are not these things that are being said about you, then who are you?"

2 Corinthians 12:9-10 "My grace is sufficient for you, for my power is made perfect in weakness, so that Christ's power may rest on me... For when I am weak, then I am strong."

Every Woman

April 1, 2010

I am every woman,
Independent, strong, and free,
Who knows that in
Surrender lies
Eternal victory,
Who will not bow to mankind's ways,
Who will not compromise.
We see God's
Holy, righteous peace
Reflected in her eyes.

I am every woman
Who has stood against a fist,
Who has held a child to her breast
and prayed,
Father guard them
from this wicked world,
Shield them from the lies,
Guide them safely through this night,
Help them see your hope and love
Reflected in my eyes.

I am every woman
Who will not bow to cruelty,
Yet surrender daily to my God
Those things that would destroy me.
I an brave, I am bold, I am beautiful,
I am here.
I have come through thunderous darkness
To dance with God at dawn,
Here in the stillness of the night
I look for God and find him waiting,
and in the quietness of prayer,
I am blessed.

When faced with adversity, who are you? What do you want the world to see in you: the person who wronged you and the injustice done to you, or your God and your faith?

The Carpenter's Son

I think about Mary, Joseph, and Jesus a lot. What must their lives been like. Knowing the cross and God's purpose there.

This drawing was meant to depict Joseph and Jesus perspectives. Joseph looking forward, in the background, Christ's earthly protector.

Christ is depicted as young, innocent, playful, and always, with His eyes turned toward Heaven.

Wishing you Hope in the morning,
Joy in the moment,
and Victory through surrender.
karen

CPSIA information can be obtained at www.ICGtesting.com
Printed in the USA
LVOW080839120213

319651LV00001B/4/P